CHRISTIAN SCIENCE TREATMENT

THE PRAYER THAT HEALS

CHRISTIAN SCIENCE TREATMENT

THE PRAYER THAT HEALS

ANN BEALS

The Bookmark
Santa Clarita, California

Library of Congress Control Number: 2001119338

Beals, Ann.
    Christian Science treatment : the prayer that heals /
by Ann Beals. -- 1st ed.
    p. cm.
    ISBN 0-930227-31-X

    1. Christian Science--Doctrines. 2. Prayer--
Christianity. 3. Spiritual healing.   I. Title.

BX6950.B43 2002   289.5
                           QBI01-2013 51

Published by
The Bookmark
Post Office Box 801143
Santa Clarita, California 91380

CONTENTS

INTRODUCTION

As the world moves into the twenty-first century, there is coming about an unexpected event — one taking place in the heart of a very sophisticated scientific and technological society. Many are turning to prayer in time of great need and learning that it has a very beneficial effect on their health and happiness, their affluence and longevity. The simple prayer of supplication, a faith that all things are possible to God, has a very definite effect on one's life. However, when such prayers are based on faith alone, one cannot be absolutely certain that his prayers will be answered.

What is needed is a more advanced form of prayer. Prayer in Christian Science is far more than one of blind faith. It is a scientific prayer that rests on a divine Principle. When this Principle is understood, prayer is no longer guess work; it is a scientific concept that one can turn to with confidence that healing can and will take place.

This new approach to prayer originated with Mary Baker Eddy, the Discoverer and Founder of Christian Science. It is called a Christian Science treatment. A concise outline of this treatment was never given in Mrs. Eddy's writings. She gave this outline of treatment to the early workers in the Christian Science movement to use in teaching students and healing patients. After learning of the treatment, I assumed that some of Mrs. Eddy's students must have written about it in detail, thus recording it for posterity, but no amount of research has turned up any notes or papers on it. For some reason it was considered a secret form of prayer, and was only taught to those Christian Scientists fortunate enough to have a teacher who recognized its value. In this way, it was handed down by word of mouth for nearly a century, being given in classes held on the more advanced teachings of Christian Science. I had at one time believed that all teachers taught about the treatment, but I later learned that many did not do so.

In my opinion, any form of prayer that can heal and bless humanity belongs to the world. There should be nothing secretive about it. Such was my conviction when the treatment was first given to me in class, and the passing years have only deepened my desire to share it in written form.

I have experienced the healing power of this prayer so often that Christian Science is a way of life for me. I never think of turning to anything else for help. When I am faced with a problem, I work it out through the study of the Bible, Mrs. Eddy's writings, and the treatment.

I was healed in Christian Science at a very early age. When I was eleven months old, I had an illness the doctors could not diagnose or cure. I was in a coma and appeared to be passing on when my mother in desperation called a Christian Science practitioner. This dear woman came and sat beside my bed and prayed for me until I regained consciousness. Within a few days, I was healed. Although I do not remember this healing, it brought my family into Christian Science. My father, Harry Smith, eventually became a very dedicated Christian Science practitioner, teacher, and lecturer.

Because of this healing and many others, I grew up loving Christian Science and its healing promise. I studied it. I lived it. After I was married, I became active in the Christian Science Church. When my children were very young, I had class instruction with Neil Bowles, of Atlanta, Georgia.

My two weeks in class marked a turning point in my life. Among other things, I was given the six footsteps of treatment. This simple outline barely covered a page in my notebook, but it proved to be the greatest tool for understanding and demonstrating Christian Science that I have ever found. I was deeply impressed with the treatment because it gave order and direction to my study of Christian Science. It was a guideline for praying — something specific to work with. All that I share with you in this discussion has been developed from this simple outline.

At the time that I learned of the treatment, I had a great need for it. I seemed to have many problems — discordant relationships, illnesses, lack. Altogether, they seemed overwhelming, and I had little hope of resolving them. I felt imprisoned in an unhappy life with no way out of it.

I was told in class that I should work with the treatment one hour each day. At first I found it difficult to concentrate ten minutes on spiritual ideas, especially with my life so filled with problems and with the daily demands of family life. Sometimes days and even weeks would go by without my working with the treatment. But I always returned to it, because I felt somehow that it was the key to understanding and demonstrating Christian Science. It held an answer to my needs. It was hard to discipline myself to pray a full hour, but I finally could do so. I also studied many works on Christian Science, especially those by Mrs. Eddy.

As I got into this work, I found it produced very interesting results. I began to get healings. There were quick, even instantaneous, healings of simple problems like colds, flu, contagious diseases, minor accidents. I am sure these difficulties would have healed without my treating them, but they gave way very quickly to my work.

Then I began to get healings of physical problems considered incurable — asthma, allergies, nervousness, an eyesight problem, a blockage in my nose. I am sure these would not have healed without my work with the treatment.

I was most impressed, however, with the healing of negative traits of character that had been with me as far back as I could remember. Fear, timidity, criticism, resentment, depression, hurt feelings, self-will, sensitiveness — these gradually lessened and disappeared through this work. It was an awesome experience to feel some negative thought or emotion that had always seemed part of my human disposition, dissolve in consciousness and vanish as though it had never been there. Year after year, I could look back and see that great changes had taken place in my thinking through this concerted effort to understand God. I could not always pinpoint exactly when these changes occurred. For the most part, they came gradually as the result of consistent work with the treatment. As this work continued, I found that lack and discordant relationships improved, and I began to appreciate even more the power for good latent in this form of prayer.

As I became increasingly successful in my work with the treatment, I decided to become a Christian Science practitioner. In 1965, I entered the public practice, and was listed as a practitioner in *The Christian Science Journal*.

I had assumed that most Christian Scientists knew about the treatment. But as I got into the healing work, I found that most students who came to me for help, knew little or nothing about how to do effective metaphysical work in Christian Science and had no knowledge of the treatment.

I was greatly concerned over this, for I realized that the treatment — so essential to spiritual healing — was being lost. It could easily become buried in time. Such a loss would be comparable to the gradual disappearance of the healing works of early Christianity.

It was obvious that something must be done to prevent this loss. The treatment had to be recorded and shared in order to insure that this unique form of prayer would always be available to those wanting to turn to God in time of need.

My purpose in this discussion, is to give you a new and more advanced concept of prayer so that you can do your own healing work. This is the ultimate goal of the Christian Scientist. In *Science and Health* Mrs. Eddy writes, "When the Science of being is universally understood, every man will be his own physician, and Truth will be the universal panacea."

This discussion of the treatment is intended to be an aid in your study of the writings of Mrs. Eddy. The complete revelation of Christian Science is found in her textbook, *Science and Health with Key to the Scriptures*, and in her other writings. It will become apparent that the study of the Bible and works on Christian Science — especially Mrs. Eddy's writings — is the basis of a prayer that heals.

As you work with the treatment, I hope it comes to mean as much to you as it does to me.

Ann Beals
2002

Mortals may have a big belief of brain, but according to Christian Science the claim that somebody thinks blinds man to the fact that there is but one Mind, God, and consequently only one real *thinker* and one *thought*. "The Lord of hosts hath sworn, saying, Surely as I have thought, so shall it come to pass; and as I have purposed, so shall it stand." (Isaiah 14:24)

When man begins to see himself as the reflection of God, Mind, and recognizes all power from Him in whom we live and move and have our being, he has reached the highest of all endowments and fruitful of all good works. *He who is obedient to Truth has immense power for service.* The truth frees him from ignorance of his capacities and privileges. It fortifies and sustains him under all circumstances. It is here and now. Pentecostal power is always present. It is the power of Mind enabling man to do the will of wisdom, for God's biddings are always enablings. It is the power to think, to act, to speak, so that life is fruitful and joyous. It is the capacity every man possesses to act in harmony with divine power, and this is to preserve a scientific sense of being.

Nothing is truth but the absolute. We do not know anything. Mind is the only source of power. Thought is the only force. Therefore, those who have turned to the fountainhead of Being for the solution of any problem, have brought such titanic force into intelligent activity that the results may seem incredible. Principle does not require time to become itself and find true expression. Mind is causative. We reflect the ideas of Mind, interpret them to ourselves and objectify or bring out the fruit of thought. Therefore, the word of God spoken into consciousness is the seed bearing fruit after its kind.

Mary Baker Eddy

Chapter I

TREATMENT AND HEALING

Christian Science treatment is the most powerful form of intelligence on the earth today. It is a method of prayer that will meet your every need. Once the treatment is understood, it heals and protects you, overcomes seemingly insurmountable problems, renovates the inner self, and unfolds the spiritual nature of God, man, and the universe.

The study of Christian Science introduces into consciousness the spiritual laws underlying Christ Jesus' healing works. One main purpose of this Science is to establish spiritual healing on a scientific basis — to make healing through prayer practical, reliable, universal.

Healing in Christian Science involves far more than blind faith in God. Through a study of its metaphysics, we exchange faith for spiritual understanding. This spiritualization of thought results in healing.

However, students have found that reading and quietly meditating on Christian Science does not always heal deeply entrenched problems, or bring about an understanding of its more advanced metaphysics. Something more is needed, something that turns the letter to Spirit, and enables prayer to heal more effectively.

The missing element is the Christian Science treatment. This form of prayer enables you to demonstrate the full healing power of Science. In fact, *the treatment is everything!* If you are seeking a reliable approach to spiritual healing, you will find it in this unique form of prayer.

1

As you master the treatment, your healing work is no longer uncertain. It is scientific. You *understand* how to heal through prayer. To heal with such assurance, you must be thoroughly schooled in the teachings of Christian Science and in the six footsteps of treatment. Then, when you apply the treatment to specific claims of discord, sickness, and limitation, your prayerful work brings healing.

We owe the concept of this powerful form of prayer to the Discoverer and Founder of Christian Science, Mary Baker Eddy. In 1866, she discovered how healing and regeneration took place in Bible times. Her years of searching the Scriptures brought a revelation into the spiritual nature of God and man. Through this experience she was healed of injuries from an accident that was expected to be fatal. When the doctor attending her did not expect her to live, she asked to be left alone with her Bible. Reaching out to God for help, she experienced a great spiritual vision and was healed. As a result of this revelation, she found that she could also heal others through prayer. But more important, she could teach them how to heal through prayer. Realizing that she had discovered the Science of spiritual healing, she dedicated herself to bringing it to the world as Founder of the Christian Science movement.

Over the past century Christian Science has healed millions. It has healed every kind of discord and disease, and in some instances it has overcome death. Many of these healings have come about solely through the study of the Bible and Mrs. Eddy's writings, especially the Christian Science textbook, *Science and Health with Key to the Scriptures.*

The treatment enables you to do your own healing work. In times of great need, you may turn to another Christian Scientist for prayerful support. But you should not depend on another to work out your problems for you. This succeeds only to a point. We all eventually reach a place in our spiritual progress when others can no longer do this healing work for us. We must do it for ourselves. Spiritual understanding is of God, and we each must find it in our own way. Through study and treatment, we gradually spiritualize consciousness until the healing and prevention of discord through prayer become a way of life. We learn to control evil and prevent it from causing discord and illness. To understand God through an inner rapport with Him, does more than heal. It enables us to transcend mortal mind and find our true selfhood in God's image and likeness.

In time, you may find you can heal others and help them to find Christian Science. The explanation of treatment is given mainly to help you learn to heal yourself. But if you cherish the desire to help others, you should begin by spiritualizing your own consciousness and healing yourself. Once you succeed in doing your own healing work, it is a very simple matter to use this same healing method to help others.

A successful treatment heals. It makes Christian Science practical. However, this intelligent form of prayer is not easily developed. We learn the art and Science of healing as we learn any worthwhile achievement — through years of dedicated work. We cannot ignore daily study and prayer when things are going well, and turn to them only when there is a desperate need for healing. Christian Science cannot be used like a 'metaphysical pill.' It is an intelligent, scientific, profound system of ideas, and those who understand spiritual healing study it as a Science.

Treatment is very serious work. You learn to heal only when you are willing to give to Christian Science the time and effort required to understand it. It is encouraging to know, however, that you do not have to study it for years before having healing results. From the time you take up the treatment, it begins to heal you. The truth found in Christian Science is a powerful thought-force. When you make it active in consciousness, it begins to neutralize the ungodlike elements within and brings to light the Christ-consciousness. Each time you pray, you do something to the inner self to

3

spiritualize it. Daily treatment brings to the surface false beliefs embedded in consciousness and destroys them. Some erroneous beliefs heal quickly, and some are so deeply entrenched that it takes many treatments to overcome them. But if you persist, even the most stubborn mortal beliefs will eventually yield to your work.

When you work daily with the treatment, you should have many healings from it — some of them very unexpected. As I stayed with the treatment day after day, I found that discordant situations and physical problems disappeared. I was not always aware of the healings taking place, for I had not been doing specific work to heal them. Such healings were gradual and permanent. I also found that when a certain amount of inner transformation has taken place, it brings about impressive changes in my outer experience, and my life would be greatly improved.

There were also problems, or claims, that I would consciously work to heal. I remember healing the claim of depression several years after I began working with the treatment. Frequently depression would overcome me, and the days would seem black with futility and hopelessness. At such times nothing seemed to help. After learning of the treatment, I would work with it as best I could. I would also open *Science and Health* and read it. Although the words had no meaning, I would read on. Soon some word or sentence would light up with meaning, a little inspiration would penetrate the darkness, and the depression would begin to lift.

As I kept handling the belief of depression through study and treatment, the periods of darkness disappeared completely. I attribute this healing to my daily work with the treatment, for this prayerful work created a reservoir of spiritual ideas in consciousness. When I needed help, reading the textbook made the truth active in thought. It set into motion the spiritual ideas that I had been cultivating in my treatment each day, and this broke the mesmerism and freed me.

Mrs. Eddy once wrote, "Mind is the only source of power. Thought is the only force. Therefore those who have turned to the

4

fountainhead of Being for the solution of any problem, have brought such titanic force into intelligent activity that the results may seem incredible." You draw on this "titanic force" with your treatment. The healing results of your metaphysical work are evidence of the infinite good that can unfold through scientific prayer.

The purpose of treatment is to gain an understanding of God and your relationship to Him. The effect of successful treatment is healing. Your spiritual understanding is measured by your healing results. Healing is evidence that you are working correctly. If you are not getting healing after a reasonable length of time, then you should examine how you are working, or perhaps work a little harder. Mrs. Eddy emphasized the need for healing in Christian Science. She once told her students, "Faith without works is the most subtle lie apparent. It satisfies the students with a lie, it gives them peace in error, and they can never be Christian Scientists without that faith which is known and proved by works."

When your goal is to learn how to heal through prayer, you go beyond the habit of analyzing problems and adjusting to them, and you begin healing them. As we learn about Christian Science, we are prone to give much thought to uncovering and dissecting mortal mind, or animal magnetism — perhaps more in others than in ourselves. But human analysis, judgment and rationalization do not heal. Mortal beliefs must be uncovered through treatment, and destroyed by the truth which uncovers them. This healing process enables you to detect and destroy subtle forms of animal magnetism that seem to be a normal part of consciousness: lack, sickness, disease, discordant relationships, hereditary beliefs, false traits of character — every mortal, material law and limitation that claims to be mesmerizing you. When such beliefs are destroyed through scientific prayer, you experience healing.

We cannot escape the work of spiritualizing consciousness. We think our way into heaven. There is no other way into it. With Christian Science, we have the means for reaching this perfect state of mind. It comes through our own study and prayer.

5

Such work not only heals you; it heals the world. Whether your prayerful work results in some impressive accomplishment, and it could; or it makes a healer of you, which is likely; or it is cherished in a quiet way, creating a very spiritual life where you are, it always affects the mental atmosphere around you. It radiates a healing influence that goes forth to bless all whom your thoughts rest upon. With this work, you do not have to be involved in humanly good activities and causes in order to help mankind. Your daily treatment will leaven world thought and heal it by the very fact that this truth, this "titanic force," is active in consciousness.

Consistent prayerful work is the greatest contribution you can make towards helping humanity. Never underestimate the value of silent prayerful work as a healing force in your life and in the world. Mrs. Eddy tells us, "Every Christian Science treatment is accumulative; the work goes on to bless all mankind. Error is nonscientific thinking, and scientific or true thinking is all that is needed to destroy it."

Before explaining the footsteps of treatment, I want to remark on several subjects that will help to lay a good foundation for the treatment. I will explore first, the spiritual age; then the three laws underlying spiritual healing; and last, the spiritual and material viewpoint. This will be followed by a thorough explanation of a general treatment.

The writings of Mary Baker Eddy are basic to your work with the treatment. Each footstep of the treatment can be traced directly to passages from her published works. Often her statements can illumine a subject with spiritual insight that she alone can give. Not wanting to quote continuously from Mrs. Eddy throughout the book, I have compiled a list of references from her published writings in an Appendix. It would be helpful to study these references in relation to each chapter as you come to it.

Chapter II

THE SPIRITUAL AGE

Christian Science is more than a religion. It is a *scientific discovery* — the most advanced scientific discovery known to man. With treatment, we are using prayer to pioneer the development of a very advanced intelligence, and are bringing to light a spiritual age. In the third edition of *Science and Health*, Mrs. Eddy referred to this present era as "the medieval period of metaphysics." The world is re-discovering the power of prayer. With the treatment, we are exploring a new thought process that will eventually revolutionize universal consciousness.

We can compare the present early development of the spiritual age to the beginning of the scientific age. The Western world began to emerge from the Dark Ages when men such as Copernicus, Sir Francis Bacon and Galileo began to discover scientific order in the universe. They did not *invent* this new knowledge. Their work did not *make* the universe scientific. Creation had *always* rested on a scientific foundation. These early scientists *discovered* facts about the universe that had always existed. Throughout all time and space, atoms, electrons, evolution, gravity and the speed of light have been present. These great thinkers were the first to discover that the universe has a scientific dimension. They opened up a scientific age that completely transformed man's mental image of all things.

During the twentieth century, the natural scientists passed through the scientific limits of creation, and found no final material cause for creation. Instead they have discovered another dimension, an intangible realm beyond and beneath the physical universe. The world is pressing against this new dimension in an effort to understand it. Is it mental? Is it spiritual? To the materially darkened mind, it remains for the most part a great mystery. But to the spiritually enlightened mind, it becomes transparent. Through Christian Science, we enter this realm and begin to live in it.

Christian Science accurately defines its structure and contents. Mrs. Eddy went beyond the veil of matter and discovered the spiritual nature of man and the universe. Just as creation has always been scientific, so creation has always been spiritual. Through her writings, we are able to understand this unseen realm and draw upon its healing power. But to do this, we must make a thorough study of Christian Science and master the method of prayer that spiritualizes consciousness.

In your work with Christian Science, you are not fighting against material forces and laws with a prayer of blind faith. You are not trying to demonstrate mind over matter. You are not struggling to achieve healing in spite of the seeming power and reality of evil and matter. Nor are you working to transform man and the universe from matter to Spirit. *They are already spiritual. They have always been spiritual.* All you are trying to do is understand what is in this fourth dimension of Spirit. You are developing a very advanced form of intelligence — one that has great healing power.

Christ Jesus, the Scientist

Christian Science is the divine intelligence expressed by Christ Jesus. In *Science and Health*, Mrs. Eddy wrote: "Jesus of Nazareth was the most scientific man that ever trod the globe. He plunged beneath the material surface of things, and found the spiritual cause." His works were not miracles, but the result of an understanding of the spiritual realm. He knew exactly what he was doing. The master Christian was so deep into the spiritual realm that his works seemed quite normal to him. He thought in a different dimension from the rest of the world. He lived on the same earth we do, but inwardly he saw it differently. He discerned the hidden structure and nature of the universe and man.

Christ Jesus taught this divine intelligence to his disciples, but their understanding of it was very limited. Ever the compassionate teacher, Jesus said, "I will pray the Father, and he shall give you another Comforter. . . He shall teach you all things, and bring all things to your remembrance, whatsoever I have said unto you." Because of this promise, Christianity has remained for centuries in a state of perpetual expectancy, and so it has always been open to the unfoldment of new ideas, always evolving towards an understanding of the scientific and spiritual dimension. First came the discovery of a scientific dimension, and now the natural scientists have discovered a spiritual dimension to creation.

Christian Science — A Scientific Breakthrough

When Christian Science is properly related to the progress of mankind, it is seen as the basis to the spiritual age, for it is the nucleus of an entirely new form of knowledge. Mrs. Eddy discovered the spiritual nature of man and the universe. She did not contrive or invent another philosophical viewpoint of God and man. She discerned spiritual laws that have always existed. She gave humanity a scientific system of ideas that correctly defines the dimension of Mind. Mrs. Eddy's great genius lay in her ability to explore the spiritual dimension, and then explain her vision in a language that others could understand.

What has she given us? To sum it up: first, she defines the spiritual nature of God, man and the universe; second, she explains the unreality of evil and matter; third, she develops a system of study and prayer through which these facts can be proven by heal-

9

ing and regeneration. These truths are scientific because they are facts about the spiritual realm. We will find in time that an understanding of this realm must come through these fundamental facts.

In giving Christian Science to the world, Mrs. Eddy was the revelator of Truth to this age. It is important to recognize her place in history, for then we believe that her books contain the Word of God. If we doubt her spiritual destiny, we doubt her writings, and this skepticism prevents us from understanding Christian Science. Christian Science is so different from our present structure of knowledge, that we must begin by having faith that it is the Truth. What we are seeking is spiritual understanding — an advanced form of intelligence. We cannot contrive or conjure up from our own limited minds something that is in advance of everything we have ever known. Spiritual understanding is a gift from God. It unfolds in the form of new ideas appearing as our own thoughts. A doubting, skeptical mind is not receptive to God's ideas, and so it cannot be taught by Him. If we are critical of Mrs. Eddy and doubt her writings, we place a large obstacle in our path Spiritward, because our minds are closed to ideas that are different from the opinions and beliefs we presently know.

There have been many efforts to discredit Mrs. Eddy and her discovery. She is still misunderstood and criticized by many who know little or nothing about her. An understanding of Christian Science includes a proper respect for its Discoverer. If we lovingly accept her place in prophecy and believe that what she has written is the Word of God — even if we do not understand it yet — then we are in a receptive state of mind, and God can teach us. God alone imparts the meaning of Christian Science. Others can tell us what they think it means, but God alone unfolds the ideas that illumine consciousness with spiritual understanding.

If we want to understand Christian Science, we must not doubt Mrs. Eddy, or her discovery, or try to mix it with other philosophies or metaphysical systems. During the years that I was a Christian Science practitioner, I was never able heal those who wanted to adulterate Christian Science, or who argued that it wasn't any different from other philosophical or metaphysical teachings. I couldn't heal them because I couldn't reach them. They were so intent on belittling Mrs. Eddy and reducing Christian Science to the same level as other teachings that this denial of the Word prevented them from finding healing. These experiences proved to me how important it is to acknowledge Mrs. Eddy as the Revelator of Truth to this age.

Mrs. Eddy herself recognized this fact. She once told a student, "People seem to understand Christian Science in the exact ratio that they know me and *vice versa*. It sometimes astonishes me to see the invariableness of this rule." Again she said, "When a student loses the true sense of me, and what I do, he is at the threshold of the plunge so many take into darkness, believing that darkness to be a greater light."

The more we understand her and accept her as divinely appointed to bring to the world Christian Science, the easier it is to understand her revelation, and to place both in proper context with the present age.

As you press deeper into the spiritual dimension, you learn that Christian Science is not in conflict with world progress. It is a vision that is many years ahead of the times. It is the *avante garde* of world thought. It is divine intelligence that enables you to understand the spiritual realm and make full use of its healing power.

The scientific age has transformed men's lives through reason and enlightenment. The spiritual age will bring about the millennium through prayer and healing.

Chapter III

THE THREE LAWS OF SPIRITUAL HEALING

You will understand the importance of studying Christian Science and praying scientifically once you are familiar with the laws governing spiritual healing. These laws are also found in my booklet *Scientific Prayer*. This booklet explains the subjective nature of prayer and how to lay the groundwork for giving a healing treatment. I recommend a study of it as part of your work with the treatment.

The healing process of Christian Science rests on three fundamental laws:

1. *Your thinking determines your experience.*
2. *Your thinking can be spiritualized through an understanding of God.*
3. *This improved thinking must then manifest itself in an improved state of existence.*

Let us examine the very simple but profound law: *Your thinking determines your experience.* This statement is the opposite of what we have been conditioned to believe. It would seem that external causes such as fate, chance, circumstances, heredity, matter, material law, economic conditions, etc. control our lives. But in Science, you learn that your thinking is the cause of all that shapes your experience. Your life is your inner self objectified. Your thoughts move forth and create your experience. Everything that exists as part of your life first exists as part of your mind. This law applies to all human experience, whether the individual is aware of it or not.

In Christian Science, a mortal, material state of mind can be exchanged for a higher form of consciousness through study and treatment. Thus, we have the second basic law of spiritual healing: *Your mind can be spiritualized through an understanding of God.* Time spent each day in study and prayer can renovate the inner self. Thought is never so hardened that it cannot change. Mortal illusions are never so fixed that they cannot be made to yield to spiritual enlightenment. Even the most deeply entrenched beliefs in discord and disease can be overcome through this prayerful work.

Study and prayer renovate the mind. When this inner change occurs, then healing must be evident through the third spiritual law: *Improved thinking must manifest itself in an improved state of existence.* Because it is a fact that your thinking determines your experience, this law works to your advantage as you progress spiritually. An improved state of consciousness *must* move forth to heal and regenerate your outer experience.

Second Law Basic to Healing

Of these three laws, the second law is the crucial one: Your thinking can be changed through study and prayer. Healing demands a change of thought, and your work with the treatment changes how you think. It spiritualizes consciousness. It produces a gentle chemicalization of thought through which the mortal, material view fades out and the spiritual view unfolds in its place.

As you do metaphysical work daily for yourself, you should sense a shifting or change taking place in consciousness. When this change takes place, it results in healing. Quite often you will know you are healed before there is any visible evidence of it. From this you learn that all healing takes place entirely within your own mental atmosphere. It is internal, or inner-directed. The best word

13

to use is *subjective. All prayer and healing are subjective. Every kind of adversity, discord, limitation, sickness, and disease begins in your own consciousness, and all healing takes place there.* With Christian Science treatment, you free yourself of the thoughts that produce limited, hurtful, sick, discordant experiences. As these thoughts are eliminated, your life becomes one of health, happiness, and abundance. Therefore, in your treatment each day, you are working to achieve one thing — a change in how you think.

This shifting within — this slow but steady mental shifting is at the heart of your healing work. It is an indication that healing is taking place. This overturning of thought comes through the inflow of new ideas and the slow dying out of mortal beliefs. You learn to give up old thought processes and hew out new ones. You develop a spiritual understanding of God through a constant chemicalization in the inmost thoughts. If you are experiencing inner change in your daily work, then you are spiritualizing consciousness, and this is all you need to realize healing and regeneration.

Importance of the Treatment

This constant change comes mainly through treatment. It has been my experience that Christian Science treatment alone produces a sufficient amount of chemicalization to spiritualize consciousness. That is why I say that the treatment is everything. We can study Christian Science for years, but as a rule study alone does not bring the needed mental change that overcomes the whole of mortal mind. It is the actual work of treating the mind that frees it of mortal beliefs and unfolds your oneness with God.

Successful treatment actually begins with the study of Christian Science. Spiritual transformation begins here. Study itself is a free form of treatment. It unfolds ideas you need to work with in treatment. You cannot read Mrs. Eddy's writings too often, or ponder them too much. But study alone is not enough to overcome all of the animal magnetism in consciousness. You need something stronger, something more concentrated and intense — a mental effort that will actually chemicalize thinking and change it. For this, you use the treatment.

The whole purpose of study and treatment is to bring about a flow of spiritual ideas that re-forms consciousness, and brings continuous change or regeneration to the inner self.

Making Time for God

There is one all-important factor for experiencing a flow of spiritual ideas — and that is *time*. You must make time for God, because *all healing begins here.* You need to be still and listen from within in order to hear the "still, small voice." This requires enough uncluttered, uninterrupted, unpressured thinking time in which to listen for God's voice. You have to make time and space in consciousness for new ideas to unfold. God is always talking to you from within, but you must take the time to listen to Him. Healing takes place in your quiet time alone with God. If God is to teach you, He has to be able to reach you. It is not possible to grab a little time each day from a busy life to read a little Christian Science and 'do' a quick treatment, and expect to make any spiritual progress. Successful metaphysical work requires a total commitment.

You should do your prayerful work in a quiet, receptive state of mind. Healing and regeneration depend on a change of thought and a change of thought depends on the unfoldment of spiritual ideas — ideas that God alone can give you, and *will* give you, *if He can reach you.* To be successful in your healing work, God has to become more and more the focal point of your thinking. Then, when you are still and listening, He speaks to you from within through a steady flow of spiritual ideas.

You need quietness to discern these ideas; and when they appear, you must be still and help them to become established in your thinking. When these ideas first unfold, they are very fragile. They are small intuitions or insights into Truth that are new and wonderful, and you need to take care of them, for they come into a mental atmosphere that has many elements foreign to them. There is a great deal of mortal mind even in the best of us. If you do not protect these ideas and nurture them until they become established, the animal magnetism in consciousness will cause you to forget them, and they will be temporarily lost. If you remain quiet and hold to them until you are accustomed to thinking in them, they become yours forever. In this way, you lay down a strong foundation of spiritual understanding within.

Work with the treatment begins with making time for God, and in reading and praying in a quiet, receptive state of mind. Through it, you are working to realize the truth set forth in *Science and Health*. With study and prayer, the letter is transformed into Spirit, and some new insight into Truth is present that was not there before.

Spiritual ideas unfold in the form of an advanced intelligence or new knowledge. They enlighten and heal the inner self as they appear subjectively through prayer. As you work to spiritualize consciousness, as you make time and space within for God to reach you, His ideas become concrete realities to you. This causes a gentle chemicalization to take place. The error within dissolves and your spiritual selfhood comes to light. As you nurture these ideas and expand upon them, it is a law that this improved thinking must move forth and manifest a more harmonious life. Thus, the three laws of spiritual healing operate scientifically to transform your whole being.

I hope that you are beginning to understand the nature and scope of this metaphysical work.

Chapter IV

THE SPIRITUAL AND
MATERIAL VIEWPOINT

The purpose of the treatment is to reveal the laws and qualities of the spiritual dimension, so we can draw intelligently on its healing power. Basic to this work are the two viewpoints presented in Christian Science. Mrs. Eddy gives opposite viewpoints of man and the universe: the material and the spiritual. She does not say there are two universes — one material and one spiritual. Nor does she say that there are two types of man — one mortal and the other immortal. She says that there are two *viewpoints* of creation and man, or two opposite mental images of the same thing. The view you have, whether spiritual or material, is wholly subjective — an image in mind.

Mrs. Eddy specifically refers to these two views in *Science and Health*, where she writes of St. John, "The Revelator was on our plane of existence, while yet beholding what the eye cannot see, — that which is invisible to the uninspired thought. This testimony of Holy Writ sustains the fact in Science, that the heavens and earth to one human consciousness, that consciousness which God bestows, are spiritual, while to another, the unillumined human mind, the vision is material. This shows unmistakably that what the human mind terms matter and spirit indicates states and stages of consciousness."

Here we see two separate states of mind. Mrs. Eddy defines them in opposite terms — good and evil, Truth and error,

Spirit and matter, reality and unreality, immortal and mortal. Since God, Spirit, is All-in-all, then evil and matter are unreal. In other words, the spiritual view is the right one and the material view is the wrong one. This complete separation of the two views is at the heart of our work with the treatment. Our goal is to understand the spiritual, and free the mind of the material view. It is possible to do this because Christian Science actually defines the spiritual nature of God and man, giving us a transcending view with which to replace the present material view.

It would be impossible to cast off the material view if, by so doing, we are left with a vacuum within. We must have something new to put in place of the old. If we are going to change how we think, we must have another mental image to change to — one that is more advanced than our present structure of knowledge. With Christian Science, we are given a spiritual view that is so complete that it becomes a new form of intelligence, replacing that which we now call intelligence. As we understand the spiritual view, we exchange our material images of man and the universe from the material to the spiritual.

This inner change is not too much to expect. Over the centuries all progress has come through a change in how men think. When men believed the world was flat, they were imprisoned by this view for fear of falling off the edge of the earth. It was a purely mental prison, completely self-imposed through ignorance. When they changed their inner image of the earth, they were free of this limitation.

When Newton, Darwin, Einstein, and other great scientists made their discoveries, they did only one thing — they changed the mind's mental images. Nothing more. While their discoveries affected certain areas of knowledge, Mrs. Eddy's discovery affects the whole of human consciousness. As we understand Christian Science, we exchange erroneous, material thought images for spiritual images of reality, and this transforms the inmost thoughts.

Two Views of Creation

To exchange the false view for the true one, we first need to define these two opposing views.

The Material Viewpoint: Because of the present scientific and humanistic philosophies, we have a material view of creation. We see man and the universe through a darkened, materialistic, negative consciousness. This godless viewpoint has been developing for centuries, until it is now concrete conviction. As a result, we believe that the universe and man are created by mindless, material forces that are cruel, harsh, cold, unfeeling, void of intelligence and love. They are defined as mass and energy, electricity, magnetism, gravity, chemistry, natural law, physical cause and effect, etc. No intelligence is attributed to these mindless forces, and man seems to be at their mercy. He believes he is governed by probability, chance, fate, circumstances, material cause and effect. This viewpoint has become a form of scientific knowledge so sophisticated that it has completely mesmerized world consciousness, and so darkened it that those who believe it seem totally estranged from God.

This negative view is a godless mental image in which mankind is presently imprisoned. It is so ingrained in consciousness that the world thinks in it effortlessly. Mankind has accepted this wrong view as "truth" because it rests on scientific laws. Based on human reason, assumption, and information gathered through the five physical senses, it is a temporary form of intelligence that will change as man's understanding of the spiritual universe replaces it.

When we think in the material view, we image it forth as our lives, and we reap the negative effects of it. All sickness, disease, discord, lack and limitation are the effects of this erroneous assumption that man and the universe are material.

The Spiritual Viewpoint: Until we begin to study Christian Science, the material view is usually the only view we have. But Christian Science introduces into consciousness a transcending view. It adds a spiritual dimension to all things and accurately defines the laws, energies, qualities, nature, contents and structure of the spiritual dimension. It defines God as the only cause and creator. It reveals the spiritual nature of the universe. Christian Science shows that the universe is wholly good, that man is spiritual, and that the real forces underlying reality are divinely intelligent and loving, for God is All-in-all. This Science goes on to show that evil and matter are powerless and unreal. They do not exist outside of the false images held by the erring human mind — images which seem to imprison man in a physical body, a mortal life, a material universe.

Here we have two views. How do we know which viewpoint is the right one? We know that Christian Science presents the right view because it gives us a powerful new knowledge, one that material knowledge has never given us — an understanding of how to heal through prayer alone.

These two views are complete opposites, and produce opposite effects. One results in negative, harmful thoughts and effects; the other has positive, healing thoughts and effects. They are such opposites that we cannot have both views in the same mind at the same time. If we refuse to give up the material view, we cannot understand the spiritual. As the spiritual view unfolds, it eliminates the material view. Through the treatment, we are consciously working to exchange the false view for the true one.

Establishing the Spiritual View

In exchanging viewpoints, you are not trying to transform the universe from matter to Spirit. *It is already spiritual.* You are in the spiritual universe right now. Look around you for this is it.

You are not trying to make yourself into the image of God. You *are* that image right now. Your goal is to put off the material view by understanding the spiritual. To exchange one view for the other, you need the treatment. In your study of Christian Science, you probably accept the spiritual view theoretically and intellectually. But this does not free the mind of the material view. This false view is so deeply entrenched that years of study in Christian Science — without the treatment — does not prove very effective in overcoming it. Thought is spiritualized only through long, hard, persistent mental work with the treatment.

It is the actual work of praying that brings into consciousness the spiritual view. Treatment is the catalyst, the tool, the means through which you transcend the old view and replace it with the new. This inner renovation is gradual. To build a strong foundation of spirituality within, God's ideas must unfold and become established in consciousness day-by-day.

As an illustration, let's compare the material view to a bottle of black ink that is so opaque no light can shine through it. If you begin adding pure water to it drop by drop, the bottle will overflow, the ink will gradually become so diluted that eventually you will be able to see through the bottle. Even so, the material mind, as yet untouched by any knowledge of Christian Science, is very dark, opaque. But as this truth is assimilated daily through "precept upon precept; line upon line," this same mind will become a clear transparency for truth. Daily metaphysical work, like drops of pure water, cleanses consciousness of the material view, as the spiritual view unfolds to replace it.

Exchanging One View for the Other

As we study Christian Science, we become increasingly aware of these two viewpoints. Then in treatment we affirm the spiritual view, while denying and rejecting the material view. The wonder of Christian Science is that it offers this choice. We each have one mind to think with; and now with Christian Science, we can choose where we are going to put our mind — either in the material, mortal, personal viewpoint or in the spiritual, immortal, Godlike viewpoint.

With the treatment, we can exchange the false for the true, but we should take care not to assume that we have already demonstrated the spiritual view unless our healing work is proof of this. We can study Christian Science for years and be so well versed in the letter that we may believe we already understand the spiritual viewpoint. But this is not always the case. When I was in the practice, I had patients who had been in Science for years, and they found themselves facing serious challenges. Yet when I tried to tell them what they needed to know for healing, they were so familiar with the letter of Christian Science that they would say to me, "Yes, I know, I know." But if they really understood these ideas, they would not have had claims to meet. We should not assume we know these truths unless our healing work proves we do. Such assumption brings with it an inflexible state of mind that resists any change, and then we really have a problem.

When we admit to ourselves that we do not understand very much about the spiritual nature of God and man, then we approach our metaphysical work with such humility and receptivity that God can reach us. It does humble us to realize that we measure our spirituality by our healing works. We understand God only to the degree that we can heal.

The spiritual and material viewpoints become more clearly defined as we work with the treatment. This form of prayer is the method through which we first separate these two views and then replace the false view with the true view. This is really what treatment is all about.

Chapter V

THE PRAYER OF AFFIRMATION
AND DENIAL

Christian Science treatment is a very unique form of prayer — a prayer of affirmation and denial. In times of need, rather than rely on blind faith in God, you take the initiative and deny a material, mesmeric illusion and replace it with the spiritual fact. You are engaged in an internal struggle to reject all that is ungodlike, while realizing the truth about God and man. You strive to put out of thought the material viewpoint and establish the spiritual.

This prayer is powerful and practical. As you develop the ability to reject the false view and establish the true view, you no longer depend upon others for healing. You can rely on your own prayerful work.

With treatment, you use prayer to transform the inmost thoughts. You counteract, neutralize, and destroy the animal magnetism within. You overcome mortal emotions, material beliefs, and false traits — all that is unlike God. You exchange faith for understanding. You move ever deeper into the spiritual dimension, and discipline yourself to be mentally obedient to God's laws.

In the prayer of affirmation and denial, you affirm the truth about God and man. You argue *for* the fact that God is All-in-all, that man is His image and likeness, and the universe is governed by spiritual cause and effect. You argue *against* the material view. You deny all belief in animal magnetism, matter, and mortal mind. You work to destroy all that claims to originate in animal magnetism or mortal mind.

23

Such treatment chemicalizes thought. When you affirm the truth and deny animal magnetism, carefully thinking of the meaning of these declarations, you de-mesmerize consciousness. You replace the material view with the spiritual. You discipline yourself to think in the Christ-consciousness and to reject the antichrist. This is the prayer of affirmation and denial.

Treatment Illustrated

This form of prayer is illustrated in the "Scientific Statement of Being" found on page 468 of *Science and Health*. Here the statements of affirmation and denial are clearly set forth: "There is no life, truth, intelligence, nor substance in matter [denial]. All is infinite Mind and its infinite manifestation, for God is All-in-all [affirmation]. Spirit is immortal Truth [affirmation]; matter is mortal error [denial]. Spirit is the real and eternal [affirmation]; matter is the unreal and temporal [denial]. Spirit is God, and man is His image and likeness [affirmation]. Therefore man is not material [denial]; he is spiritual [affirmation]." This is an excellent example of the statements of affirmation and denial found throughout Mrs. Eddy's writings. With this simple prayer of affirmation and denial, we begin to demonstrate Christian Science.

The prayer of affirmation and denial was used daily by Mrs. Eddy and the early workers in the Christian Science movement. Those who were called to serve in her home, and to do metaphysical work for the Cause, were often given specific instructions on how she wanted the work done. Many of these treatments were recorded, and eventually a number of them were compiled by Gilbert Carpenter, Jr., in a book entitled *Watches, Prayers, Arguments*. The following short treatments are taken from this book:

Inasmuch as I am God's child, spiritual, and not material, I must be perfect. I am whole; I am free; I have all I need every hour; I am without fear, without anxiety; I live in Spirit, not in matter (error); I am not in danger; no one can harm me or deprive me of any good. I know no such thing as pain, suffering, or disease, for I am a reflection of Life, Truth and Love. I am never disappointed or grieved. The harmony of my being is never broken, because I live in the Infinite. No condition of the body is essential to my happiness, for God, good, only, is the spring of all my joys. My life is hid with Christ in God. Therefore I am immortal, for nothing can be lost or die in God.

Divine Love fills every avenue, flows through every channel, and removes every obstruction. There is one infinite Mind and that Mind is my Mind and governs me. All my thoughts come to me from this Mind and return to their source. In this Mind there is no material sense, no other mind, no mortal mind to tempt, to harm or control. Know this, realize it, and you are master of the occasion, of yourself and others.

You are the child of the loving God, surrounded by infinite Love. There is no hatred or evil to frighten you. You have no disease, you have nothing to fear, you are not in danger, you are entirely well, and continually held in the presence of God.

Such treatments could have a great spiritualizing effect on your life if you worked with them each day. They show how Mrs. Eddy brought the truth in direct contact with human needs, and used it to resist animal magnetism and realize God's allness. She taught how to argue for the good in consciousness and against the evil.

Affirming and Denying

This form of prayer is also referred to as 'the argument' in that you argue for good and against evil within your own consciousness. Think about the words *argue, declare, resist, realize, affirm, deny*. They denote mental action. When you argue against or resist evil and affirm or realize the truth, you are doing something mentally to how you think and feel. You are de-mesmerizing consciousness and defending yourself against the aggressive mental suggestions of animal magnetism. You are counteracting mortal mind by making the truth active within.

The treatment is an instant avenue to the healing power of prayer. Whatever the claim, you can handle it immediately. If you are confronted with an illness, you can take the initiative, instantly resisting all suggestions of the symptoms, and realize the indestructible nature of your health. If you are faced with a discordant or hateful situation, you can quickly deny this false image of man and affirm that man reflects divine Love. If you lose something, you can argue against the erroneous suggestion of loss and insist that the one Mind knows where everything is because nothing can be lost to omniscient Mind, nor to you as Mind's reflection. If you are in danger, you can deny all fear and belief in evil as a reality, and affirm that your life is safely hid with Christ in God, beyond all threat of harm or danger. Whatever the false suggestion, the prayer of affirmation and denial is ever with you as a way for overcoming or preventing all claims of discord and illness.

Please realize, however, that if these simple statements of Truth are used like a formula, they will not be very effective. They must mean something to you. The healing power of a short treatment is successful only when it is backed up by daily metaphysical work with the general treatment.

If your thinking controls your experience, then the more you spiritualize your thinking, the more effective your argument is when you face a challenge. When you give at least one hour each day to the treatment, these shorter treatments bring quick, even instantaneous results.

Through consecrated work with the general treatment, it is easier to "stand porter at the door of thought," as Mrs. Eddy instructs us to do. When thought is one with God, you are alert to the aggressive mental suggestions of animal magnetism. You can quickly recognize and handle all suggestions of sickness, lack, discord, adversity, confusion, dishonesty, accident, stress, limitation, sin, disease, death. In this way, you "pray without ceasing," and learn to control what takes place in your experience.

Daily devotion to your metaphysical work not only heals and protects you, but it brings unplanned, unexpected good into your experience. And it gives you the ability to heal others.

Daily Treatment

The prayer of affirmation and denial is the basis of the treatment. The general treatment is the one used in your quiet time alone with God. In order for short treatments to be effective, they must come from the spiritual understanding that has unfolded in your daily work with the six footsteps of a general treatment. A short version of treatment will not always heal and protect you unless you spend time each day working with the general treatment. You will need daily practice with the treatment if you want to become accomplished in the art of healing.

The treatment not only heals and protects you, but it is the means through which you begin to transcend the belief in a mortal life and a material body. Such an experience comes only through a great devotion to the mastery of the whole of Christian Science.

Too often we do not try to demonstrate Christian Science until we are in great need. We may even turn to it as a last resort. When we put off the treatment until a crisis is upon us, we are already under such a strong claim of animal magnetism that we are being forced to pray. The mind is in a very darkened state, and we are trying to get out of a suffering experience and back to what we call normal. We are fighting an extremely aggressive mesmeric condition. When we have overcome it, we have merely returned to the same state of mind that we had before the claim appeared, with perhaps some spiritual lessons learned from the trial. Very little spiritual progress is made under these circumstances. We do not do our best work in a sick or disturbed mind. Sometimes, if we have neglected our daily work with the treatment, we have great difficulty in realizing healing.

If we want to emerge from the material, mortal dream, we must pray when we are in our very best state of mind. When we are not under the mesmerism of sickness, pain, fear, stress, and anxiety, we can think more clearly. Then our metaphysical work carries us beyond our present state of consciousness into a more spiritual state of mind. If we are dedicated to Christian Science, we will study it simply to know God better. We will not wait until a problem forces us to pray. Our best moments of inspiration and spiritual growth usually take place in the heart of clear, calm prayer. Through this daily work, consciousness is gradually illumined with a spiritual understanding that is profound, strong, effective, and we find a closeness to God that comes only through this total commitment to Him. Daily study and prayer are absolutely essential not only to healing, but to the spiritualization of consciousness that totally transforms the inner self.

The Six Footsteps of a General Treatment

The treatment is not a complicated maze of metaphysics. It is simple, practical, and very effective. As it is explained step by step, it will take shape as an intelligent approach to prayer, one that is basic to understanding and demonstrating Christian Science.

Briefly, the six footsteps are as follows:

1. *Protect your treatment. This identifies it and prevents animal magnetism from annulling and reversing it as you are giving it.*
2. *Affirm God through the synonyms by relating the synonyms to each other. This footstep is focused entirely on God.*
3. *Affirm the spiritual nature of man and the universe by relating them to the synonyms. (The second and third footsteps are the affirmation part of treatment.)*
4. *Deny animal magnetism. Deny matter, mortal mind, evil, malicious animal magnetism, and specific claims. (The fourth footstep is the denial part of treatment.)*
5. *Affirm the oneness of God and man.*
6. *Protect your treatment so it cannot be annulled or reversed by animal magnetism after you have completed it.*

This outline is an orderly form of prayer, but it is not intended to be a formula. Your daily work should not become a rehearsal of familiar statements of Truth. If you are striving to understand God, He will always be unfolding new and inspiring ideas for you to work with. For this reason, the treatment cannot become stereotyped. God directs it. Because God reaches you through the unfoldment of ideas, you must take great care not to become too rigid in your treatment. Stay flexible, open to change. When new and inspiring ideas unfold, they need to be accepted, nurtured and established in consciousness. If you are too determined in following these footsteps, you may not take time to accept these ideas and make them your own. You need to do all six footsteps thoroughly as

29

often as possible, but you should not be bound to this outline. It is only a guideline for daily prayer.

In order to do your best work with treatment, you should read Christian Science constantly. Study the Bible, Mrs. Eddy's writings, and other worthwhile works on Christian Science. Reading Science supplies you with ideas to use in praying. Actually, there are two parts to this work: the study of the letter, and the prayerful work that converts the letter to Spirit and heals.

Chapter VI

FOOTSTEPS ONE AND TWO
OF A GENERAL TREATMENT

Reforming a mind accustomed to human, mortal thinking, and disciplining it to think spiritually, is a great challenge. But through study and prayer, you can gradually come to think in spiritual ideas with greater ease than you now think in mortal, material beliefs. The treatment brings about this reformation or renovation of the inner self.

The treatment is so important that each footstep will be covered thoroughly in the coming chapters. They will explain the basic treatment to be used each day in doing metaphysical work for yourself. As you become familiar with the general treatment, you will be able to adapt it to meet specific problems.

First Footstep: Protect your Treatment

You should begin your treatment by protecting it. This first footstep is brief. It is meant to identify, establish, and defend your work. Mrs. Eddy once wrote, "Every treatment must include the understanding that it is the Mind of God; it cannot return void, and it cannot be reversed by any so-called law of malpractice or human belief."

In protecting this work, you can silently declare that you are giving a Christian Science treatment; it is the Word of God and the truth about God and man; it cannot be reversed or annulled by animal magnetism. Malicious malpractice cannot make or prevent it from accomplishing its purpose.

You should also identify Christian Science with Mrs. Eddy, and Christ Jesus with a statement that acknowledges Christian Science as the promised Comforter, discovered and founded by Mary Baker Eddy. You can also declare that it is the Science of Christianity based on the teachings of Christ Jesus, the Way-shower.

This first footstep is not long or involved, but you can include any thought you feel should be added to this example.

Second Footstep: Affirm God through the Synonyms

The second footstep is the foundation of a healing treatment. The main purpose of treatment is to understand God. To the degree that you understand God, you understand the spiritual nature of man and the universe. This spiritual understanding makes obvious the unreality, the nothingness, of evil and matter. The second footstep is positive in its declarations of truth. It comprises the major part of the affirmative footsteps of treatment, and is usually the part of treatment that requires the most time.

This footstep should begin with one of the three definitions for God found in *Science and Health*. On page 115, Mrs. Eddy defines Him as, "GOD: Divine Principle, Life, Truth, Love, Soul, Spirit, Mind." On page 465, she writes, "God is incorporeal, divine, supreme, infinite Mind, Spirit, Soul, Principle, Life, Truth, Love." In the "Glossary" on page 587, she gives this definition: "GOD. The great I AM; the all-knowing, all-seeing, all-acting, all-wise, all-loving, and eternal; Principle; Mind; Soul; Spirit; Life; Truth; Love; all substance; intelligence."

You can begin the second footstep by prayerfully affirming one of these definitions, and then follow it by relating the seven synonyms to each other. Before we take up the synonyms, let's consider the whole of God in terms of His allness and nearness.

God's Allness

With the treatment, we are trying to understand God, the only cause of all things real, and the scientific nature of the spiritual dimension. Christian Science reveals what is in this unseen realm. God is in it. He is all that is in it. There is no other cause or presence or power. God alone is the only cause and creator.

God is not a physical being existing in some remote time or place. Neither is He abstract or unapproachable. He is All-in-all, the one universal Father-Mother, God. He consciously creates and sustains the universe and man, and He is inseparable from all that He creates. He is not centered in any one place, or identified with any specific time. He exists everywhere, all the time. He expresses infinite intelligence, love, beauty, law, harmony, perfection, goodness, wisdom, justice and mercy everywhere, all the time. Therefore, He is here and now the very foundation of our being. He is *omnipresent*.

God is *omnipotent*. His power for good is the only power there is. His allness excludes the presence of any other power. While it may seem that the universe and man are created by material forces, they are really created and sustained by the power of God. The power in the spiritual dimension is not material, harmful, cold, inanimate, harsh, or cruel, but spiritual, harmless, warm, kind, gentle, and good. God's thoughts and actions are never harmful, discordant, or negative. They can only bless and heal.

God is *omniscient*. His divine intelligence is everywhere present, everywhere active, everywhere law to man's being. The intelligence of Mind is the conscious process that creates and governs man and the universe. God is self-perpetuating, self-sustaining, self-expressing. He is without limit in intelligence, power, and excellence.

The divine Mind is forever expressing itself in action, unfoldment, creativity. God is not passive or inert. He is intimately

33

involved in every detail of His creation. Mrs. Eddy uses very active verbs to describe God: operates, influences, bestows, controls, pardons, rewards, pervades, blesses, makes, delivers, unfolds, acts, leads, inspires, illumines, designates, casts out, dispels, produces, creates, gives. Actually, God is *omni-action*. He maintains law, order, beauty, goodness, harmony, and perfection in His creation.

In looking through the visible universe to the cause underlying it, we find that the *only* cause is God. Without His divine intelligence, presence, and power, creation would cease to exist. The real power causing and sustaining the visible universe is Spirit, not matter. As we accept these spiritual and scientific facts about God, the spiritual dimension begins to take on form and meaning.

Keep in mind that there are not two universes — one material and one spiritual. There is just one universe and one man which are the effect of one Mind. When we realize these facts about God, we are developing a right understanding of His handiwork.

In the spiritual dimension, there is one God, one cause, one creator, one Father-Mother. God fills the spiritual realm. In other words, the spiritual dimension is inhabited by one Mind. An understanding of this realm draws us closer to the Father, as it reveals to us that we are, throughout eternity, one with Him.

These statements are very elementary, but as simple as they are, they demand much prayerful thought before we convert them from theory to concrete conviction or realization. We may believe them and have faith in them, but how little we understand them! The purpose of the treatment is to make these facts so real to consciousness that they replace the illusory material viewpoint.

The purpose of your daily treatment is to enable you to know that God is All, and to *know* you know. When the allness of God is an absolute fact to you, it destroys the material viewpoint, and any belief of evil as being real or powerful.

God's Nearness

If God is All-in-all, He is as close to us as our thoughts. The allness of God destroys the belief that we can ever be separated from Him or exist in a material universe or mortal life. We cannot go beyond His presence and power.

The treatment does away with the myth that God does not know anything about us. Because God does not know evil or matter, Christian Scientists sometimes insist that God cannot know you or me because we are mortals. This assumption is inconsistent with the teaching of God's allness. Nowhere in her writings does Mrs. Eddy state that God does not know anything about us. True, He does not know evil, but we are not wholly evil. We are, in reality, God's reflection or expression, and so we are inseparable from Him.

Christ Jesus taught of God's nearness. He said, "I and my Father are one," and "Your Father knoweth what things ye have need of, before ye ask Him." From his spiritual viewpoint he understood that he was one with God.

This idea of God being very near, "a very present help in trouble," dispels the belief that God is off in some distant time and place. By His very allness, He is right here, right now. In *Unity of Good*, Mrs. Eddy writes of this spiritual oneness, "Because God is ever present, no boundary of time can separate us from Him and the heaven of His presence; and because God is Life, all Life is eternal."

Mrs. Eddy taught her students to think of God as very near. Many statements attributed to her, and recorded by her students, illustrate this. The following are found in *Divinity Course and General Collectanea*:

God sees in man the perfect reflection of Himself. God's thoughts of us are unchanging.

Love is the very nearest thing to us all the time. We can always bring God to us instantly by declaring He is with us. We never reach out for Him in vain. God has ordained for us all good, and He will remove our sins from us as far as east is from the west, when we want to give them up.

God is always with a good desire, giving it power, activity, energy, intelligent action and rich fruition. He brings every right endeavor to its fulfillment, and gives more blessings than one has sought.

God is your refuge and a strong deliverer. He will hide you under His wings till the storms are past and the sunlight of His presence cheers and invigorates you with new strength and vigor.

God has placed us all in our orbit, and like the stars, we are held there by His power.

God is giving each of us the experience best adapted to lead us to Him.

It is Love, unquenchable Love, that loves you better than you can love yourself; Love that cares for you every moment and will not leave you comfortless.

God is with you and God is Truth. So you have it, Truth right with you every hour, and [you] never can be without Truth, and Truth is telling you just what to say and what to do, and how to do all that is good.

Mind plans every detail of our affairs.

Statements like these prove that God is ever here and near. It is important that we understand our closeness to God, because through the erroneous assumption that God doesn't know anything about us, we reject God, exclude Him from our mind, deny our own oneness with Him, and in so doing, we block out our inner rapport with the Father.

When we assume that we are unknown to God or that God

cannot be known, He seems so vague, impersonal and far away, that we can't turn to Him with the conviction that He hears our prayers and answers them. This belief of separation is a lie. It is the biggest of all lies. One of the greatest changes that the treatment brings to our basic image of God and man, is God's nearness to us — indeed, our oneness with Him. Paul wrote, "In Him, we live and move and have our being." We are already one with God. Our treatment simply reveals this to us. As we grow in Christian Science, we find an ever-deepening awareness of His presence, proving that we are inseparable from Him. This divine presence is so good, warm, loving, kind, gentle, intelligent, and wise, that we learn to trust God and turn to Him for everything.

When we deal directly with the false assumption of God's aloofness, we change the viewpoint of our relationship to God, for we discover our oneness with Him as an established fact throughout eternity.

We must understand and accept God's nearness and allness, because we are entirely dependent on Him for the ideas that we must have to spiritualize consciousness. Consider this fact carefully. We cannot invent or devise the spiritual viewpoint out of the darkened, materially mesmerized mind we now have. The spiritual view unfolds through God's thoughts appearing to us subjectively. Through the treatment we cultivate a rapport with God from within. His thoughts unfold to us as concrete ideas. He teaches us through the appearing of His thoughts to the inner self, and He can do this because He is as close to us as our thoughts. Daily He imparts ideas that we can understand and use where we are in our spiritualization of consciousness.

To experience this unfoldment or this flow of ideas, we must have absolute faith that this source outside of ourselves is near to us and can reach us. As we pray, believing that God hears us, we begin to feel God's presence subjectively. As His thoughts unfold, we exchange the material view for the spiritual.

Thus, when you pray, you are not alone. God is present waiting for you to reach out to Him, to make time and space in consciousness for the unfoldment of His ideas. You pray not to an unknown God or to a God afar off, but to a God that watches over you with tender, loving care, unfolding each phase of your spiritual progress.

In *Unity of Good*, Mrs. Eddy tells us, "Now, this self-same God is our helper. He pities us. He has mercy upon us, and guides every event of our careers. He is near to them who adore Him." Thus you learn of God's close relationship to man — to you.

Ponder these two words, *allness* and *nearness*, in discovering your relationship to God. These are only two words of many that Mrs. Eddy uses to define God. She also defines Him as incorporeal, supreme, infinite, eternal, harmonious, merciful, just, perfect, pure, good. If you will make a list of all the words used for God in the textbook and study them one by one, they will take on great meaning. Then when you make your affirmations and denials in treatment, the words mean something to you, and this prayer with understanding is what heals.

As you work with the synonyms, many insights into God's nature unfold. But you should also keep in mind the whole of God as Father-Mother; consider His closeness, warmness, and goodness; His anticipation of your every need; His ever-presence brooding over you, caring for you, teaching, protecting, loving you. As you understand God's allness and nearness, you sense God as a pulsating, thinking, feeling presence with you throughout eternity.

Affirming God's allness and nearness is a good beginning for a treatment. It leads into the main purpose of this second footstep, which is declaring God through the seven synonyms.

Chapter VII

THE SEVEN SYNONYMS

In the definition of God, Mrs. Eddy gives seven synonymous terms: Principle, Mind, Soul, Spirit, Life, Truth, Love. These synonyms are the foundation to treatment. They are the key to the structure and nature of the spiritual realm.

The seven synonyms are like a spectrum. When light passes through a prism, it is separated into many colors. When God is defined through the synonyms, we see spread before us many qualities of His infinite, divine nature or individuality.

Each synonym has certain attributes that define it in a way that distinguishes it from the others:

> *Principle is law.*
> *Mind is intelligence.*
> *Soul is identity.*
> *Spirit is substance.*
> *Life is being.*
> *Truth is reality.*
> *Love is power, relationship.*

The treatment revolves around the synonyms, and your healing talent depends on how well you understand these seven terms for God. To give a thorough treatment, you should study each synonym carefully, and learn how to relate the synonyms to each other. Since these terms for God are the very essence of treatment, you should make a special study of each of them.

Principle

Principle is law. God's laws give scientific, moral and spiritual stability to the universe and man, because they are governed by the divine Principle, Love. These laws are absolute. Because God is Principle, we live in a universe of law, order, plan, and unity.

The spiritual dimension is a divinely structured system of spiritual qualities and laws, governed by a Principle that is undeviating in its power and control, constant in its nature.

Spiritual laws never change. We live in a spiritual universe governed by a perfect system of divine laws. These absolute spiritual laws are comparable to the laws of the physical universe. The natural sciences are based on physical laws, such as chemistry, gravity, and hydraulics; and we derive much good from being able to understand and use these laws.

In Christian Science, we go beyond the physical universe and its laws, into the underlying spiritual realm and its laws. In discovering the structure and content of the dimension of Spirit, we find moral and spiritual laws based on the divine Principle, Love.

In learning the true nature of reality, we begin to understand the source and origin of both the physical and spiritual laws of being. Because the natural laws of the physical universe are reliable, we have a stable and predictable universe — one we can understand. Even so, because God is Principle, we have a stable and predictable spiritual dimension — one that we can understand. We have absolute moral and spiritual laws of right and wrong to live by. We have, for example, the law of intelligence, the law of Love, the law of honesty and integrity, the law of Life, the law of divine justice and mercy.

We hear today of everything being relative. The theories of relativity and probability originated in physics, but they have been used to lower the moral standard of the Western world. They have challenged the Ten Commandments and Christ Jesus' Sermon on the Mount. But the laws found in the Scriptures were not of human origin. They can no more be changed than the laws of chemistry. These laws are absolute and eternal because they are of God. The power to heal through prayer is in proportion to our obedience to these spiritual laws. They cannot be shelved, but must ultimately be understood and obeyed.

The divine Principle is not a cold, hard, mechanistic, material law-enforcer. Principle is neither physical nor mental, but spiritual — a warm, intelligent thought-force. It creates and governs all things through laws that are wise, loving, good.

The law of intelligence, the law of Love, the law of inexhaustible good, the law of harmony and perfection — these never change throughout eternity, because their divine Principle never changes. These laws exist and govern all things right here, right now, whether we know it or not.

Principle governs the unfoldment of God's orderly plan for the universe and man. Dynamic creativity is itself a divine law of infinite progression. Each idea unfolds according to God's plan, and each idea has its own place and purpose in that plan.

There is one system of laws governing one divine plan, unfolding man and the universe in perfect order. The laws of Principle give unity, order, plan and stability to God's creation.

All of mankind's suffering, adversity and limitation come from defying these laws. Even though we may disobey them ignorantly, nevertheless they are as absolute as the law of gravity. We cannot disobey them and not pay the penalty.

Spiritual healing never violates God's laws. All suffering comes from ignorant or willful disobedience to divine laws, and healing comes from understanding and obeying them. The suffering and discord of mortal existence will cease when we understand Principle and obey its laws.

As you can see, this synonym alone begins to reveal the true nature of God. Mrs. Eddy said a great deal about the laws of

God, and the so-called laws of matter and mortal mind. Your work with the treatment enables you to distinguish between the two.

There are many words that define Principle, such as: cause, basis, causation, originator, maker, creator, source, origin, fountain-head, essence, intrinsic, subjective, primary, law, order, plan, unity, completeness, relationship, indivisibility, oneness, wholeness.

Each attribute expands upon your understanding of God as Principle. Then when you declare, "God is Principle," the statement has great meaning. You believe what you are affirming to be true, and this conviction is what heals.

There is much more I could give on Principle. But in order to keep close to our subject of treatment, I will only give a short analysis of each synonym.

Researching the Synonyms

You will need to research each synonym for yourself. This in-depth study of all seven synonyms is very important to your treatment. Christian Science is so vast a subject that it sometimes seems overwhelming. The six footsteps of treatment give order and direction to your study.

After I learned of the treatment, I took each synonym and spent a month working with it. I researched it in the concordances, to the Bible and Mrs. Eddy's writings, the dictionary, and the Roget's Thesaurus. The dictionary was helpful for often I found that I really didn't know what a word meant. The Thesaurus gave many words that related to each synonym — nouns, verbs, adjectives. The Bible and Mrs. Eddy's writings then gave the spiritual interpretation for each.

As I worked with each synonym, and focused my daily treatment on it, the synonym began to take on new depth and luster and meaning. This method of orderly research simplified my studies. I learned to take one main subject at a time and work with it until I had a better understanding of it. This work gave me a foundation of spiritual understanding that I could not have found otherwise. When I think, "God is Principle," all that I have learned from this research gives the statement power and meaning.

After you study the synonyms and their attributes, you can go on to other subjects covered in treatment: man, universe, creation, mortal mind, matter, animal magnetism, evil. If you do a thorough study of these, you will understand the statements you make in treatment, and your prayer will then transform consciousness and enable you to do impressive healing work.

Mind

Mind is intelligence. The spiritual dimension has a system of laws that expresses divine intelligence. By adding this unseen dimension to creation, we add an intelligent dimension to it. The presence of divine intelligence, or a thinking cause, permeates all time and space. God, Mind, is a living presence, and so the substance of being is pure intelligence. If God is divine intelligence, then there is no fate or chance in reality; no mysticism in it; no thoughtless, ignorant, harmful material forces in it; no mistakes in it. All is a manifestation of the intelligence of divine Mind. The cause of all things is not found in matter and its laws, but in the intelligent thought-forces of the one Mind. This intelligence is not evil, cruel, cunning, crafty or shrewd. It is divinely wise, warm, gentle, pure, and good.

Christ Jesus embodied a mental atmosphere of intelligence so pure, so uncontaminated by mortal beliefs and material laws, that he had extraordinary success in healing. He must have had an unobstructed rapport with the one Mind, an uninhibited receptivity to God's thoughts, as he walked on the water, stilled the storm, multiplied the loaves and fishes, healed the sick, raised the dead.

Now, as then, this intelligence takes the form of specific

ideas. In your work with treatment, you should experience a flow of divinely intelligent ideas within, whereby you draw upon the inexhaustible resources of Mind for your own needs. Visualize yourself submerged in a realm of infallible intelligence, expressed as clearly defined ideas, so that all that exists is a manifestation of divine intelligence. This intelligence is expressed in consciousness as ideas unfolding to you as your own thoughts.

From this atmosphere of intelligence, this reservoir of divine wisdom and understanding, of creativity and originality, come spiritual ideas, creative ideas, intelligent ideas, practical ideas. These ideas are not vague or mystical, but ideas clearly defined to meet the needs of the moment. Where we have questions, God has answers; where we have needs, God has supply; where we wonder, God knows. God is the source of every answer to every need.

We draw upon this divine intelligence through our treatment. God works subjectively, through the unfoldment of ideas. The treatment is the most active channel through which these ideas or intuitions reach us. Treatment develops spiritual intuition. It brings divine revelation. As we pray, visualizing this divine realm of ideas and expecting unfoldment, ideas appear which bring us spiritual growth and meet our human needs right where we are. At one time, these ideas are not known to us — and then they are. At one time, they are not in our consciousness — and then they are. These are God's thoughts becoming our thoughts.

As divine ideas come into consciousness through prayer, the spiritual viewpoint unfolds, develops, stabilizes and is expressed in healing and increased good in our lives. Thus, Mind is a very important synonym to work with, for quite often it is not only inspired love, but inspired intelligence and wisdom that we most need for healing and spiritual progress.

When you experience this inspired flow of ideas, you then realize how near God is to you. As you work with Mind, you feel your intelligence growing, your thought expanding. By

44

acknowledging God as the source of all ideas, of all intelligence, and then knowing that you reflect this infinite intelligence, you heal the belief of limited intelligence.

Pray over the synonym Mind. Study it carefully. As you do, you will become conscious of Mind always with you, an ever-present help, divinely infallible, healing, protecting, blessing you, giving you every good thing. Mind has many attributes, such as intelligence, wisdom, understanding, logic, enlightenment, perspicacity, discernment. I do hope you will make this synonym one of the first that you research and focus upon in your daily work.

Soul

Soul is identity. Attributes for the synonym Soul include ego, identity, and individuality. Soul is the opposite of sensualism. It is spiritual sense as opposed to the five material senses. True identity originates in Soul, which is expressed in the beauty and individuality of all things, giving to each idea its own unique identity.

Soul gives to man his true individuality, which embodies the Soul-like qualities of creativity, originality, sensitivity, vision, intuition, beauty, graciousness, loveliness, poise, refinement, spontaneity, warmth, joy, humility, purity, innocence, wit, and humor. Your real selfhood expresses these Godlike qualities naturally, effortlessly. As the expression of God's being, man reflects all of the qualities of Soul, and you are that man.

God's work is never perfunctory, mechanical, repetitious, mundane, common, or routine. It is inspired, exquisite, original, esthetic, and magnificent. Each thing is distinct with an identity of its own, yet each blends into a perfect whole. Observe the world of nature — the glorious sunset, the rose in the early morning dew, the little cluster of mushrooms, the nightingale's song, the winter landscape in the moonlight. This beauty and perfection does not happen by chance. It is the work of God unfolding inexhaustible beauty, harmony, and perfection to His universe.

The infinite resources of Soul create a universe that is dynamic. All things real originate in Soul and unfold as tangible ideas in an infinite variety of shapes, forms, and colors — all expressions of God's thoughts.

Our Soul-senses reveal the universe in its spiritual transparency and beauty. We hear the Word of God as the "still, small voice." We feel His presence and power as divine Love.

Soul unfolds spiritual vision and intuition to us, transforming the inner self, for Soul is the synonym that reveals reality to us. Soul, or Mind, is the origin of the spiritual ideas that come to us as inspiration. At one time, these ideas are not there — they are unknown; and then these ideas are present — they are known.

When these ideas illumine consciousness for the first time, the activity of Soul is bringing to light our true selfhood. Through them, we experience our own revelation of Truth. This revelation first appears as inspiring, Soul-like intuitions. Such insights unfold to each of us our own revelation of Truth. This revelation unfolds as intuitions or ideas that correctly define the spiritual nature of God, man and the universe. They are spiritual revelation individualized in consciousness. When they first unfold, they come as fragile spiritual thoughts that are new to us. As we make them our own, they become a natural part of our thinking. They are the advanced intelligence we are seeking.

As these intuitions continue to unfold, they shape our true individuality in God's likeness, changing our viewpoint from the material to the spiritual. We become aware of the esthetic qualities of Soul, and see the universe and man as God made them. We discern the beauty, harmony, and perfection that have always been the basic attributes of Soul.

There is, of course, much more to Soul. I have only touched on the special things that it means to me. Soul is a challenging synonym to work with. Research such words as revelation, vision, intuition, unfoldment, beauty, creativity, identity, individuality, harmony, perfection, grace, loveliness, inspiration, poise, temperance, humility, purity, innocence. I am sure you will find many other attributes for this beautiful synonym.

Spirit

Spirit is substance. The substance of Spirit replaces the false image of matter, and matter disappears from consciousness, for Spirit proves the unreality of matter. The material viewpoint claims that life originates in dust or nothingness, and is evolved by the non-intelligent forces of matter. The five senses deceive us into believing that all life is at the mercy of the thoughtless forces of material laws. But Christian Science gives a spiritual viewpoint of creation. The one cause of the universe is not material or mental, but spiritual. All atomic structure and behavior is governed by Spirit, not matter. In transcending the material view, we do not destroy the atomic universe; we translate it by discerning the cause of it to be spiritual.

Spirit creates, governs, and cares for all things throughout eternity. The loving, intelligent energies of Spirit are strong, gentle, harmless, and indestructible. As we study Spirit, we look *through* the universe and man, and discern underlying them the divine laws and thought-forces of God. In *Miscellaneous Writings*, Mrs. Eddy writes, "Christian Science translates Mind, God, to mortals. It is the infinite calculus defining the line, plane, space, and fourth dimension of Spirit."

Adding a spiritual dimension to the universe, spiritualizes our image of it. As this dimension comes to light, matter fades out, for we cannot have both viewpoints in the same mind at the same time. As we see creation complete with a spiritual dimension, creation becomes Godlike. We discover that we are in the spiritual universe now, governed by spiritual laws, created and controlled by Spirit, God. We cannot live outside of or beyond the influence of this one perfect cause, for God is All-in-all. The hidden realm of intelligent, ever-present Love is the substance of our being.

Whether we are aware of the spiritual dimension or not, it is always present, governing all things. We may believe that matter governs, but *Science and Health* states, "Spirit is the life, substance, and continuity of all things. We tread on forces. Withdraw them, and creation must collapse. Human knowledge calls them forces of matter; but divine Science declares that they belong wholly to divine Mind, are inherent in this Mind, and so restores them to their rightful home and classification."

You can research Spirit through such terms as substance, spiritual sense, spiritual existence, spiritual causation. In your daily prayerful work, you can press against the boundaries of your mind until they give way, and you discern this spiritual dimension as a concrete reality.

Over the years, I have grown to love each of these seven terms for the light they have given to my understanding of God. They bring the word *God* to life. They define His nature and individuality. They tell what He is and what He is not. And somewhere in this work, God leaves the abstract realm of the unknown and becomes a very real presence — a thinking cause conscious of our every need and always supplying it. The synonyms tell us how near and dear God is.

Life

If God and man are one perfect cause and effect, then material existence is an illusion, a myth, which comes from *not* knowing about man's relationship to God. The discord and limitation resulting from this ignorance falls away as our real life complete in God unfolds within, for man's life is a holy thing, "hid with Christ in God," governed by divine intelligence and Love.

God is Life, and Life is being. It is health, vitality, activity, joy, strength, immortality. It cannot lapse into a state of imperfection, discord, sickness, disease, age or death, for it is inexhaustible good. It is always active, always conscious. It can never be destroyed, used up, or contaminated by a false material view. Therefore, as God's idea, we cannot die. We have no choice but to live, because we can never be separated from God, who is our life. All that ever dies is a material belief or wrong view. As the material illusion of life in matter disappears, we are not left with a vacuum. Our spiritual life unfolds in the heart of consciousness, and as it unfolds it moves forth to bless us beyond anything we could humanly outline for ourselves.

Material existence would put us at the mercy of matter and its laws, material cause and effect, fate and circumstances, adversity, sin, discord, disease, death. But this is not the life God has given us. It is what Mrs. Eddy calls our "imaginary life." In *Science and Health*, she writes, "Entirely separate from the belief and dream of material living, is the Life divine, revealing spiritual understanding and the consciousness of man's dominion over the whole earth. This understanding casts out error and heals the sick, and with it you can speak 'as one having authority'."

We learn about spiritual existence through the synonym Life. It reveals a separation between a troubled, material belief of life and harmonious, spiritual life. As you experience healings from your metaphysical work, you are seeing the first real evidence of spiritual existence manifesting itself in your present experience.

At some point in your metaphysical work, you begin to discern spiritual life as a concrete reality. A chemicalization in consciousness brings about a clear separation of the mortal, material belief of life and the immortal, spiritual life. There crystallizes a very distinct awareness of your own immortal being, or Christ-consciousness. All that is mortal is on one side of this division, and all that is immortal is on the other. At this point, you know that what takes place in the mortal life can never affect your life in God, for your true being reflects perfect, indestructible Life.

As you develop this understanding, spiritual consciousness rather than mortal mind begins to govern your life. You see that divine Life is here and now, that all the good you may believe you have lost, or been deprived of, exists intact and undisturbed in your spiritual life.

What obstructs this higher demonstration of Life? Usually we are held back because we are afraid that if we let go of our material selfhood, we won't have anything to take its place. Our present structure of life is the only life we know. But as we learn to yield up belief in material existence, our spiritual one replaces it.

Both the material and the spiritual view of existence cannot occupy the same mind at the same time. Mrs. Eddy tells us in the textbook, "A great sacrifice of material things must precede this advanced spiritual understanding." Through our metaphysical work, we let go of the material view. Then our spiritual life emerges in practical, healing results. Day-by-day we see increasing evidence of God's care in every detail of our life. Spiritualization of consciousness is a gradual thing. As we press against the boundaries of the mind and break through the hardness of materialism, we discern as tangible reality the spiritual life that God has given us.

As your work with the treatment unfolds, you will see that the renovation of the inner self brings to light Life, and you find your own spiritual selfhood as a complete expression of this Life. Some words relating to Life are being, eternity, immortality, health, holiness, vitality, activity, joy, bliss. These are worth careful research and study.

Truth

Truth is reality. As you understand the spiritual dimension, you have in consciousness the same divine Science that Christ Jesus knew. This Science is Truth. We read in *Science and Health*, "Truth is the intelligence of immortal Mind." Truth reveals what is real, what is true, and separates the real from the unreal.

Each time there unfolds a spiritual fact about God, man, or the universe, that fact is eternal. It is absolute Truth. It never changes or becomes obsolete. Thus, through treatment you build an understanding of reality that is factual, scientific, true. You come to think in the Truth as naturally as you now think in material beliefs. You can give up the erring beliefs of mortal mind because you have this transcending view to replace them.

Truth is summed up in these facts: God is All-in-all, the only cause and creator; man and the universe are spiritual effects of this one divine cause; matter and evil do not exist as realities; they are nothing but erroneous beliefs that are eventually destroyed through spiritual understanding. This is Truth. Anything that adulterates, compromises, or deviates from the facts set forth in *Science and Health* is not Truth.

Human philosophies, opinions, wisdom and knowledge are often mistaken for truth, but these are always changing as the evolution of human thought goes on. Such knowledge is built on false foundations that must eventually be replaced by absolute Truth.

At this time, a form of false material knowledge occupies the mind. But if you argue for the truth presented in Christian Science, and against all material knowledge, Truth will reveal itself to you and eliminate the error in consciousness.

Truth is Science. It is consistent. It never varies, never changes. It is immutable, immortal knowledge revealing itself to man. It is omnipotent, omniscient, omnipresent God.

Truth separates reality from unreality, fact from fiction, Spirit from matter. It neutralizes and destroys error. As Truth is introduced into the mental atmosphere, it produces a chemicalization that destroys the mortal view and unfolds the immortal view, for Truth discloses only what is real.

In treatment, we use Truth to destroy error. The leaven of

Truth works in consciousness to purify it, eliminate everything unlike itself, and heal the inner self. To think Truth is to make it active in consciousness, and this is the healing power of scientific prayer.

Truth is also the basis of justice, honesty, integrity, trustworthiness, reliability. A consciousness filled with Truth is naturally just, honest, responsible. As you pray daily to reflect Truth, it will reveal itself to you.

Study Truth as Science, understanding, knowledge, reality, and as honesty, integrity, justice. Think this synonym through carefully, for it is a very important one.

Love

Love is power and relationship. There is in reality only the gentle, harmless atmosphere of Love. God is Love, and this Love harmonizes, unifies, and blesses the universe and man. Love's activity is effortless, gentle, yet all-powerful. Mrs. Eddy once wrote, "Love is a mighty spiritual force." Divine intelligence, wisdom and understanding demonstrate Christian Science which is permeated with Love. The spiritual realm is void of fear and hate.

Love motivates all that God does. It is affectionate, compassionate, patient, forgiving, gentle, kind, tender, pure, merciful, just, and true. It is radiance and inspiration. Love's activity is effortless and natural, because in reality there are no negative elements to obstruct God's plan and purpose.

Because of God's love for man, man never wants for any good thing. Love's warm, tender presence is all-embracing. Love protects and sustains all that it creates. Love is the great Giver. Universal abundance is Love in action. Nothing can separate you from Love. As you understand Love, you find God so near, so at one with all that He creates, that you know you are eternally safe in His care. Love anticipates your every need, and supplies the need, and the avenue through which it unfolds. Only darkened mortal thoughts and emotions can close the channels through which God reaches you. When you understand that God is the source of all good, you can turn to Him to meet every need.

Love is a law — not just a term for God, but a universal law. Mrs. Eddy refers often to the divine Principle, Love. The law of Love is like the law of gravity. The law of gravity cannot be defied. If we go against gravity, we pay a penalty. Even so, Love is divine Principle, and the law of Love is absolute. To move into the spiritual dimension, you must love as God loves. You can understand Love and reap the good it bestows only as you are obedient to this divine Principle. When the law of Love is defied, we experience discord and suffering.

You learn to obey the law of Love as your love expands to include all mankind, and you express patience, forgiveness, kindness, generosity, gentleness, tenderness, goodness to everyone, everywhere, all the time.

God's love is holy. It never falters, never fails, is never withheld. As you study this synonym and pray for an understanding heart, you feel His closeness, caring for you, protecting you, lifting you out of mental darkness through lessons that force you to yield up dependence on material things and turn to Love alone for everything. God is not cold and aloof. He is not apart from you, unaware of your needs, uncaring, indifferent. Love is as close as your thoughts. Mrs. Eddy once told her students, "Love is the Way. Love worketh with us. It does not work with hate; hence we must love. Love 'worketh with us to will and to do,' that is, to accomplish. 'Love never faileth'; hence we cannot fail in our demonstration."

You will want to do a thorough study of this synonym, and pray for God to reveal spiritual love to you.

I have explored briefly the seven synonyms to help you begin your work with them. I cannot stress enough the need to understand these seven terms. What little I have said on them leaves much unsaid. I have shown how to research and analyze them. Each synonym has many attributes, many shades of meaning. Each one is distinctly individual from all the others; yet they all relate to each other. They blend together to define the whole of God. To succeed in healing, you must make it your business to know what they mean.

After I studied these terms one by one, giving each a long and thorough research and analysis, I used the results of my study in my treatment each day. With my thought focused on one of the synonyms as I prayed, I found that marvelous unfoldment took place in the treatment.

After I had researched the synonyms, I turned to the other subjects covered in the treatment. I also read the best material I could find on Christian Science.

This approach to Christian Science is like an intellectual pursuit of spiritual things. It is true that human intellect and reason are not the same as spiritual understanding. Spiritual understanding first comes through intuition or revelation, and then grows to conviction or realization. But with this thorough study, we are actively seeking to understand God. As you reason in treatment on Love as compassion, forgiveness, and humility, ideas will unfold that teach you what compassion, forgiveness and humility really are. As you pray for wisdom, your unfoldment will reveal the difference between human and divine wisdom, and there is a difference! There is a difference between mortal and immortal life, material and spiritual laws. This study of Christian Science, combined with treatment, reveals things that remain hidden until we make a concerted effort to know them.

I cannot emphasize enough the need for you to give an indepth study to these seven terms for God. As the structure of treatment unfolds, you will see how basic the synonyms are to this work, and why it is best to start your study and research with them.

This second footstep is concerned only with God. Animal

magnetism, mortal man and matter do not enter into it. It is focused on affirmative statements relating to the synonyms. This second footstep is the foundation of treatment, for it establishes in consciousness the nature and allness of God through the synonyms.

In using the synonyms in treatment, you can go through them one by one and affirm them as the truth about God. You can also relate them to each other. In doing this you constantly expand upon your understanding of God. A brief example of how to relate the synonyms to each other using the synonym Principle would be as follows:

Principle is Mind. All that God creates is obedient to the laws of divine Principle, because these laws are intelligent, wise, and good. They operate as divine intelligence and govern the orderly unfoldment of God's ideas.

Principle is Soul. It is a divine law that Soul must express harmony and perfection in creation. The ideas of Soul, governed by divine law, manifest individuality, beauty, grace, loveliness, harmony and perfection.

Principle is Spirit. The substance of the visible forms of the universe and man is governed by the law of Love and the law of intelligence. Therefore the substance of true being is harmless, safe, indestructible, and eternal, held in a state of perfection by the Principle that governs it.

Principle is Life. Being is governed by God's absolute laws — the law of harmony and perfection, the law of inexhaustible good, the law of immortality, the law of Love. Everything in Life unfolds according to God's perfect plan, because the one Principle creates and governs all. God is law to every living thing He creates.

Principle is Truth. Throughout eternity Truth is absolute — never changing, never incomplete, never wrong. In reality, only the spiritual laws of being govern man, and he thinks in Truth — the Science of one Principle governing all according to God's law, order and plan. Truth is divine Principle, expressing integrity, honesty, and reliability.

Principle is Love. Love is a law to the universe and man. The divine Principle, Love, creates and cares for all things with the unfaltering affection of the one Father-Mother, God. Because the law of Love is absolute, it anticipates every need, supplies it and opens the way for its unfoldment at the exact time and place that the need arises. This law is the law of Life to man, the Truth of his being, the substance of all that he has. He trusts it, understands it, and relies upon it, because he knows that divine Principle is Love — the perfect Father-Mother, God.

You can also relate the other synonyms to each other in the same way. In relating the synonyms to each other, the combinations are unlimited. Each synonym helps to define the others. As you reason on Life as Love, Mind as Spirit, Soul as Truth, these terms for God come to have great meaning. Then your metaphysical work has healing power. You begin to think in spiritual qualities and ideas rather than in personal sense, mortal beliefs and material cause and effect, and this spiritualization of thought moves forth and transforms your life. Gradually you come to understand the spiritual universe and man as a divine reality here and now, for God is truly All-in-all.

Chapter VIII

THIRD FOOTSTEP
MAN AND THE UNIVERSE

The third footstep of treatment is mainly concerned with discerning the spiritual nature of man and relating to it.

Let's review again the three laws of spiritual healing. First, your thinking determines your experience. Second, your thinking can be changed through study and prayer in Christian Science. Third, this change in consciousness must move forth and change your life.

A right image of man is essential to a healthy, happy life. If you embrace in consciousness a mortal image of man, then this false image will manifest a mortal life. If you see man as sick, dishonest, selfish, stupid, unkind, immoral, critical, hateful, cruel, or malicious, then this is your own false image. You most likely express these qualities to some extent yourself, and in so doing, you draw into your experience individuals who seem to have such mentalities. A mortal, material view of man creates a mortal, material inner self which moves forth to become a discordant mortal life. The only way to escape the lack, limitation, sickness, and discord of mortal life is to actually exchange this mortal view of man for the spiritual view.

The third footstep of treatment enables you to do this. It actually re-forms your concept of man; and each time your image changes, this new view moves forth to improve your life.

As you work with the synonyms in the second footstep, your understanding of God deepens and expands. Then in the third footstep, you relate these spiritual qualities to man. The purpose of this work is to spiritualize consciousness, to convert theory to understanding, and establish the true image of both God and man. To do this, you need to gain a better understanding of God, and at the same time, see man as made in God's image. In the treatment, you affirm powerful statements of truth about God, and then relate this truth to man, and identify with it.

Identifying with Your Treatment

In this third footstep, your statements about spiritual man are about *you*. Relate to them. Accept them as facts about yourself. I want to emphasize that this work is for yourself. As we learn to heal, we may neglect our own spiritual growth to work for the family, church, country, and world — and for those who come to us for healing. It has been implied in the past that it is selfish to focus your mental work on yourself when others are so in need of help. Actually, you have to spiritualize your own thinking before you can heal others, and this is accomplished by doing specific metaphysical work for yourself daily. Such work includes affirming the spiritual facts about God and man, and identifying with these statements by knowing they are the truth about yourself in God's likeness. Then you need to reject the error in your own consciousness with the absolute conviction that this affirmation and denial is a healing treatment for yourself. As you heal and transform your own thinking, you can do better healing work for others.

It is sometimes said about the treatment that it must be impersonal, that we must leave ourselves out of it and stay only in absolute statements of Truth. But it would seem impersonalizing this work prevents the person doing the work from identifying with it. Yet this work is very personal in that you, as an individual, are involved, affected, and changed by it. Your whole inner self is renovated. I have not found any way of impersonalizing this work, or leaving myself out of it, and at the same time realizing an inner change that spiritualizes consciousness. How can we work for inner change and at the same time impersonalize the work?

The purpose of treatment is to educate, heal, and transform the inner self. It should renovate our mental atmosphere. All spiritualization of thought begins subjectively. It comes through the unfoldment of spiritual ideas or divine intuitions in the heart of consciousness. How can anything be more personal than this? How can we experience this inspiring unfoldment if we are not seeking it for ourselves, listening for it, working for it? Through treatment, you are cultivating an understanding of your spiritual identity, your oneness with God. You are working to heal your image of man — your image of yourself.

Think about this point carefully. God doesn't need healing. He knows who He is and who you really are. So the treatment is not for Him. Mrs. Eddy said that we cannot do another's work for him. We each must do our own work. Although our work does radiate out to bless others, we cannot work out their salvation for them. The treatment has to be for the one giving it. Therefore, you should identify with the truth you are declaring.

In the third footstep regarding man, you should keep in mind that this work is for yourself. When you declare the spiritual facts about man, know that *you* are that man, that you can understand the spiritual nature of man, that you can express that man here and now. By arguing for this fact, you begin to be that man.

Through this work, the truth is active in consciousness. You produce a change or shifting within, as an understanding of man — of yourself — comes to light, and false beliefs die out. This inner change is the chemicalization that heals. This is what you are working to achieve.

It is not enough to read and study what Christian Science teaches about man. To find your spiritual selfhood, you must wrestle mentally with the hypnotic conviction that you are a mortal, created by material forces, and living apart from God. You cannot demonstrate your spiritual selfhood without the long, strong metaphysical work that drives out the false view and discerns the true one.

Who are you really? This is what you are trying to find out. In the chapter "Recapitulation," in *Science and Health*, Mrs. Eddy asks the question, "What is man?" Her answer includes this passage, "Man is spiritual and perfect; and because he is spiritual and perfect, he must be so understood in Christian Science. Man is idea, the image, of Love; he is not physique. He is the compound idea of God, including all right ideas; the generic term for all that reflects God's image and likeness; the conscious identity of being as found in Science, in which man is the reflection of God, or Mind, and therefore is eternal; that which has no separate mind from God; that which has not a single quality underived from Deity; that which possesses no life, intelligence, nor creative power of his own, but reflects spiritually all that belongs to his Maker."

The entire answer to this question, "What is man?" needs careful study. Mrs. Eddy does not say there are two men. She tells us that there are two viewpoints of man — mortal and immortal, material and spiritual, unreal and real. You are not trying to escape a material life or heal a physical body. You are not working to exchange one form of external conditions for another. You are trying to change your viewpoint of man, and this change takes place subjectively. *The total transformation from material to spiritual man takes place within your own mental atmosphere.*

Mrs. Eddy defines not only mortal man, with whom we are most familiar, but she also defines immortal man, and this is an entirely new view of man. With this definition, you have the correct image of man to put in place of the present one.

A demonstration of the correct image begins with the seven synonyms. We develop our spiritual view of man as we develop our understanding of God. The two are inseparable. We read in the textbook, "We know no more of man as the true divine image and likeness, than we know of God." Therefore, in the second footstep, we affirm God through the synonyms; and then in the third footstep, we declare man through the synonyms. In this way, the spiritual concept of God and man unfold together. Our affirmations about God precede our declarations about man, for God is cause and man is effect. In the third footstep, all that we have affirmed to be true about God, we affirm to be true about man.

Relating Man to the Synonyms

The synonyms reveal man in God's likeness. We find this man as we relate him to the synonyms, for he reflects all the attributes of God. Following is an example of how we can relate man to the synonyms:

Principle is law, order, plan, unity. God's creation is subject to spiritual laws, and so man is obedient to these laws and is governed by them. These laws operate to bless and care for him, and so he is always safe. His life has plan and purpose; it is an orderly unfoldment of good. Each individual is an indispensable part of the perfect whole of God's plan, and man is at one with all that God creates. What blesses one, blesses all under the law of Love. God's laws bless you to the extent that you understand and obey them. Obedience to God's laws results in healing and regeneration. As God's idea, you can know and obey these laws and be blessed by them.

Man is one with *Mind*, divine intelligence. Mind includes an infinity of ideas; and man, immersed in this atmosphere of spiritual ideas, naturally reflects the intelligence, wisdom, and understanding of Mind. All that Mind knows, man knows by reflection. Spiritual ideas, unfolding as man's being, come through his oneness with God. Man thinks in the mental atmosphere of Mind. It is the only mental atmosphere he has ever known. It is filled with the ideas of the one Mind, which constitute man's intelligence. This Mind is your mind by reflection.

Soul is the source of man's identity or individuality. Soul gives grace, beauty, creativity, poise, wit, and humor to man. Soul reveals the spiritual intuitions that inspire and enlighten consciousness with Truth. Your own revelation of Truth comes through Soul, for Soul imparts the original ideas that reveal the spiritual nature of God and man. As you discover reality for yourself, you come to know your real identity as God's reflection, expressing the creativity, originality, beauty, grace, joy and inspiration, which is your God-given individuality.

Spirit is the very substance of man's being — his origin, source and cause. The thought-forces underlying man's being are spiritual, intelligent, and loving. As you look through what appears to be a physical man, you see, in place of the seeming physical and mortal elements, the animating presence of Spirit, Soul, for the substance of man's being is spiritual, not material. The indestructible substance of Spirit gives him eternal Life, immortal Truth, divine Love. Think about these facts. Ponder them carefully, for you are considering the nature of your own being. These statements are the truth about you.

Regarding the synonym *Life*, Mrs. Eddy tells us in *Science and Health*, "Man is the expression of God's being." Therefore, man's real life is Godlike. It is eternal, indestructible, inexhaustible, harmonious, perfect. Health is permanent. Joy and happiness are forever his. Life expresses inexhaustible activity. It is infinitely good. All that is true about God as Life, is true about man as the expression of Life — is true about you. What a different image of Life this is from mortal existence. As this prayerful work progresses, you lose your life as a mortal and find it as an immortal. Mortal life begins to fade out of consciousness as spiritual existence unfolds. In prayer, you begin to sense a spiritual life apart from and beyond material existence. It is always there, but now it begins to appear as something you actually experience — a life created, governed and sustained by God. Whatever the state of your present life, there always exists, intact and undisturbed in God, your spiritual life. Each time you declare, "God is my life," you claim as yours all that divine Life expresses: freedom, abundance, bliss, health, activity, joy, harmony, perfection, all that is good.

God is also *Truth*, reality. Truth is true knowledge or Science. As God's reflection, man knows the truth, and he *knows* that he knows it. He knows only the real or spiritual viewpoint. Truth in consciousness is pure knowledge unfolding as concrete reality. Man thinks effortlessly in this Truth or Science. Man's understanding of God makes him secure. Man is trustworthy, honest, reliable, because he is governed by Truth. He has only the single vision, the real viewpoint, which is spiritual and scientific. As you probe deeper into Christian Science, Truth permeates consciousness and becomes the very knowledge that you think in naturally. Truth can never be lost. It never changes. It becomes established as your mind, and is all that you know. To know Truth is to understand the spiritual nature of God, man and the universe, and this is reality.

Now consider *Love* as power and relationship. Man, expressing God, is always loving. Love is a spiritual law to his being. He cannot know an unloving thought or feeling. He is Love manifested. He is gentle, tender, affectionate, kind, understanding, patient, humble, and good. Love is his life. Divine Love is the power that maintains his relationships in harmony and unity. All relationships are bound together by affection and understanding. Love as our Father-Mother God, blesses man with infinite good throughout eternity, and gives man dominion over the earth.

This is a brief example of how man is defined through the synonyms. What is true about God is true about man, for they are inseparable.

As you declare these truths about man, know that you are that man! Identify with the truth you are declaring. Unless you identify with it and learn to think in it, spiritual man is little more than a theory, a myth. He does not come to life as your real selfhood. By affirming the truth about man, the truth is active in consciousness. This de-mesmerizes your thinking and breaks down mortal beliefs about yourself. It introduces into thought the spiritual view of man as God's reflection.

Practice thinking these spiritual facts about yourself, and you will begin to see yourself and others in a better light. Your image of man becomes more Godlike. In the treatment, you argue for the truth about immortal man and against the error or false belief of mortal man. You begin to think of yourself as being honest, intelligent, capable. You feel secure in Truth. You are more loving. Your spiritual selfhood begins to emerge. You express the Christ. In this third footstep of treatment, you become acquainted with who you really are — spiritual man.

Although each step of treatment is important, these two parts of treatment — affirming God and man through the synonyms — are the heart of your work. They are the key to healing and progress. The denial of animal magnetism, mortal man and matter is necessary, but it is the realization of Truth that heals.

Transforming Our Image of the Universe

In the third footstep, we can begin spiritualizing our image of the universe. We cannot transform our image of God and man, and continue to hold in thought a material image of the universe, for we then have a spiritual cause, God, and a spiritual effect, man, existing in a material universe. God and man are pitted against the godless forces of matter. These two viewpoints are antagonistic to each other, and this is not scientific. As we change our concept of God and man, we also need to change our view of the universe.

This change takes place subjectively. The transformation of thought unfolds as we pray to see the right view of creation. Although we are in the spiritual universe here and now, the spiritual view becomes a reality only as we work to discern it. This means looking *through* the visible, tangible environment we live in, and visualizing beneath it a spiritual cause. Mrs. Eddy once said, "There is no material plane. We live, move, and have our being in God, and we cannot pass out of that."

In studying Christian Science, we are going beyond the physical evidence and seeing more than what the five senses tell us. We are discerning a universal hidden thinking cause. As a simple illustration of this, suppose you received a letter written in French, and you couldn't read a word of French. To you, the letter would mean little more than paper and ink. But if you gave it to someone who could read French, instantly the paper and ink would take on a thought dimension.

This is a very simple example to help you visualize a thought dimension to the universe. To the mind unschooled in spiritual verities, the universe seems purely material. But as the spiritual realm is added to this image, the universe takes on a thought dimension. We can look through the visible, tangible universe, discern the spiritual cause behind it, and define it through the synonyms. As you define the qualities, laws, structure, and content of reality in spiritual terms, the "new heaven and new earth" of God's creating begins to appear. Man and the universe become the effect of God, and not the product of matter.

We live in a benign universe, a harmless environment, a holy place. There is not one harmful physical or mental element in God's universe. It is always at the standpoint of absolute harmony and perfection. God is the law of harmony to His own creation.

Relating the Synonyms to the Universe

In relating the seven synonyms to the universe, you can affirm that the universe is governed by the laws of *Principle*, which unify the whole of creation in one grand plan and purpose. Creation

65

is a manifestation of the ideas of *Mind*, and so is wholly intelligent and can be understood spiritually and scientifically. Underlying its visible forms is the indestructible substance of *Spirit*. It expresses God's inexhaustible creativity, for it originates in *Soul*. The universe is indestructible, for it is a manifestation of eternal *Life*. *Truth* reveals the real universe — a universe created and governed by a divine cause. It is permeated by the atmosphere of *Love*; good alone is transpiring, for Love motivates all that God is doing. All that is true about God and man is true about the universe.

In this work, you are converting your own image of the universe from darkness to light by adding a spiritual dimension to it. You are pressing through the seemingly opaque material view and developing the spiritual view, in which all atomic structure and behavior is created and governed by the divine Principle, Love. God acts through atomic form and action. Not one atom in the whole of creation can exist apart from God. Therefore, the substance of the universe is divinely good. It is the creation of Mind. When you see all substance in this light, matter vanishes. You then have an atomic universe drained of all that is material. Underlying it is God alone. Then the dual image of a material and spiritual creation dissolves, and the spiritual creation alone remains. To have this single vision of the universe, you need to give much prayerful work to this end. When you do, you begin to break the mesmeric dream of life in matter, and see instead the infinite realm of Mind.

The Affirmation Part of Treatment

Relating God, man, and the universe to the synonyms comprises the affirmation part of treatment. The second and third footsteps are positive statements of Truth that focus on the divine nature of all that really is. In affirming the Truth, you discipline yourself to think in spiritual ideas. Your mind is active in the fundamental truths of Christian Science.

As work with treatment progresses, your declarations of Truth should become strong and clear, until they begin to transform consciousness. This work reaches deep into the inmost thoughts and stirs the error within so that it can be seen and destroyed. In treatment, you are touching on holy things that few people have explored. You are discovering knowledge that has been secret since time began. When you think about it, how many have ever explored the structure and nature of the spiritual realm and used scientific prayer for spiritual healing? As you do this work, Christian Science becomes a force for good not only in your own life, but for the entire world. Your spiritual thoughts silently move forth and neutralize evil and materialism and heal world thought. The blessings that flow from this prayerful work can hardly be described.

Chapter IX

FOURTH FOOTSTEP
HANDLING ANIMAL MAGNETISM

The fourth footstep of treatment is focused on the denial of animal magnetism. In Christian Science, *animal magnetism* is the specific term used for evil, matter and mortality — all that comprises the material viewpoint. Since this view is an illusion, the purpose of the treatment is to break the hypnotic hold that animal magnetism seems to have on consciousness. When this mesmerism is broken, error disappears, and truth unfolds in its place, bringing permanent healing and regeneration.

Animal magnetism includes everything in the mortal dream of existence: evil, matter, material law, material cause and effect, all the sick, sinful, discordant, ungodlike beliefs that seem to make up the material universe and mortal man — the belief in a life apart from God.

In Christian Science, animal magnetism is defined as nothing — the imaginary opposite of God, good. It is neither person, place, nor thing; it has no presence or power. With study and treatment, you can reduce it to nonexistence. If you understand your affirmations of truth and denials of evil, you can destroy it. Evil cannot remain in a consciousness filled with Truth that denies it entrance. Truth, active in consciousness, destroys the hypnotic influence of animal magnetism; and when this hypnotic influence has been overcome, healing takes place. There is no exception to this law.

Having affirmed the truth in the first part of treatment, you must then deny animal magnetism. While affirming the truth is all important, affirmation is only part of the work you need to do. *You must handle animal magnetism.* The fourth footstep is crucial to your work. I cannot emphasize enough the need to handle all forms of evil's hypnotic suggestions..

The affirmation of truth is the major part of treatment, and an inspired realization of God's allness can certainly heal. But there are times when our best and most persistent affirmations do not bring healing, or the healing comes slowly, or it is temporary and the problem returns. Sometimes the prayerful work that heals one problem leaves another untouched. We then wonder why our healing work is not consistent. Any inability to heal usually indicates that we do not know what animal magnetism is, or how to handle it.

The only way to free the mind of the mesmeric influence of evil is through the prayer that specifically denies and destroys all belief in evil. Animal magnetism is not always met by the affirmations of Truth alone. Neither will the passing of time free us of it. Evil must be driven out by strong denial in the treatment. We must wrestle with it until we are free of its influence.

It is sometimes said by Christian Scientists that error is nothing, and so we do not need to handle it. This is a very naive approach to spiritual healing. Metaphysical work done from this standpoint often fails to heal. Our work is to *prove* that evil is nothing by actually destroying it. Only when a suffering, discordant claim has yielded to our work and is no longer present — only then can we say evil is nothing. Looking away from a problem and saying that it isn't real while it still remains, is not Christian Science. We must handle each claim of evil until we have dominion over it. Facing evil and reducing it to nonexistence is not a simple task, but to be healing metaphysicians, we must learn how to do this.

We avoid analyzing and handling animal magnetism because it is so disturbing and unpleasant. But once you experience the power that the treatment gives you over it, you will use every opportunity you have to exercise this God-given dominion.

For this footstep, I recommend that you study Mrs. Eddy's book, *Unity of Good*. Read it many times, for its profound message will give you strength and courage to do this work. In it, she explains how the allness of God proves the unreality of evil. She writes: "As God is Mind, if this Mind is familiar with evil, all cannot be good within. Our infinite model would be taken away. What is in eternal Mind must be reflected in man, Mind's image. How then could man escape, or hope to escape, from a knowledge which is everlasting in his creator? . . . Nowhere in Scripture is evil connected with good, the being of God, and every passing hour it is losing its false claim to existence or consciousness. All that can exist is God and His idea. . . All that is, God created. If sin has any pretense of existence, God is responsible therefore; but there is no reality in sin, for God can no more behold it, or acknowledge it, than the sun can coexist with darkness."

As it becomes clear that God does not know evil, we begin to grasp some idea of the power we have over it, for we see that every denial of evil is enforced by the spiritual laws of God.

Our dominion over animal magnetism begins by analyzing it. In doing this, it helps to see first its effects — that is, matter and mortal mind. Then recognize its more hidden form as cause, the whole of evil, or animal magnetism.

1. MATTER

Mrs. Eddy tells us that there is no matter, and physicists have come to agree with her — there is no matter as we think of it. Theoretically we may accept this idea, but don't we continue believing in it as real? Even though physicists have proven that there is no matter, the world goes on being subject to matter and its laws, because apart from Christian Science there is no way of de-mesmerizing the mind of this belief. But with study and treatment, we can deny matter through the synonyms and free the mind of this illusion, because we have spiritual facts to replace it.

Matter is the most aggressive form of hypnotic suggestion originating in animal magnetism. It is a solid conviction in mortal mind — nothing more. Matter does not exist as a reality. When we understand this, we are no longer governed by its laws. To prove matter unreal, we reason from a spiritual basis concerning atomic structure and action, and this changes our viewpoint of man and the universe. Mrs. Eddy does not say there are no atoms. In *Miscellaneous Writings*, she states: "Atomic action is Mind, not matter. It is neither the energy of matter, the result of organization, nor the outcome of life infused into matter: it is infinite Spirit, Truth, Life, defiant of error or matter."

With her profound revelation as our guide, we can reason that there is no solid matter, and no physical or material laws, causes, or forces in the universe and man. The ultimate cause of all atomic action is in the spiritual dimension; and this cause is Mind, not matter. Thus, we have a wholly different image of cause and effect with which to replace the material one. God and His creation are spiritual, not material. The atomic universe and man are the effects of the warm, intelligent thought-forces of Mind.

De-materializing Consciousness

To mortal mind, atomic action seems to be governed by the mindless forces of gravity, electricity, magnetism, chemistry, etc. Matter seems dense, hard, opaque. Man appears encased in matter and at the mercy of material elements. These erroneous mental images are driven so deeply into consciousness that they must be specifically handled and cast out. We can only free ourselves of this dark, disturbing mental state by replacing it with an understanding of Christian Science. To do this, we must reject the false view again and again, denying its reality, and affirming the truth in its place.

We de-materialize thought as we see through the physical universe and discern divine Mind governing all atomic structure and behavior. The laws and energies creating and sustaining the atomic universe and man are of God. He is All-in-all. This spiritual power is intelligent and loving. As we understand God and His creation from the correct spiritual viewpoint, the material viewpoint fades out, and matter becomes unreal.

In working this way, we press against the boundaries of the mind until the mesmeric belief in matter breaks down. We see the unreality of matter as we dissolve our belief in it through prayer. This mental change comes gradually, but it can be achieved to some degree here and now through strong, persistent metaphysical work.

This change takes place *subjectively*. We do not do a thing to the outer world. We simply translate our mental image from a material to a spiritual view. Such understanding comes through an unrelenting effort to break the belief in matter. Each time you challenge this belief, you de-materialize thought to some extent.

Because God is Love, there is nothing harmful in God's universe. All belief of harm or threat or suffering is in mortal mind. We *believe* we can be harmed by weather, germs, virus, heredity, animals, plants, chemicals, gravity, electricity, heat, cold, sunlight, food, exercise, diet, drugs, alcohol, and the body; and we experience pain and suffering from such beliefs because they have become solid conviction in the erring human mind. All suffering is due to what we think. Nothing more.

As we develop our understanding of God, we begin to see through matter's seeming reality. How can the harmless energies of Spirit, constituting all substance, cause a harmful material effect? Why would God as Love imprison man in a discordant physical environment? How can indestructible Life be controlled and defeated by mindless elements? In this way, we reason on the unreality of matter, challenge false convictions, and replace them with the truth. Then matter loses its reality and power, and we have dominion over it.

We each have a certain combination of material beliefs to overcome. We may believe we are allergic to certain foods, or are affected by the weather, or afflicted by an incurable physical problem. We come under the world's collective belief in matter's reality. One-by-one, we must detect and destroy the material illusions that we consciously or unconsciously harbor within.

Treating the Body

We should work to have the right concept of body. We are not trying to eliminate body, but to spiritualize our image of it. Our belief in a physical body is animal magnetism's lie about our true body. If our visible form was never tired or sick or old, then it would not be a burden to us. As we begin to see that matter does not exist and that we do not live in it, we become less conscious of our body, and less fearful about it. We trust God to care for our health. Christian Science shows that everything is mental, and so we must work out physical problems through correcting our thought. As thought is corrected, reformed and purified, our body becomes healthy, because our body is a manifestation of our thinking.

Matter — Evil's Subterfuge

As the hypnotic nature of matter becomes apparent, you learn that evil uses matter as a subterfuge. By believing in the reality of matter and its laws, you are blinded to the real cause of mortality — the hypnotic lies of animal magnetism. Evil deceives you into believing that all cause and effect are material, and are *external* to consciousness.

Don't we usually blame most of our problems on material causes — on bad weather, germs, physical malfunction, contagion and other objective conditions over which we seem to have no control? If animal magnetism can make us blame our problems on material causes and mindless physical forces, then we will never detect the real cause — *the hypnotic suggestion of animal magnetism*. If we are always coping with the effects of evil, we never trace the claims of mortality to the real cause — the mesmeric work of evil itself.

When we learn that the belief in matter is caused by the suggestions of animal magnetism, and is mental and not physical, we no longer handle effects. We go directly to the cause of the problem — animal magnetism — and handle that. Then our work has tremendous healing power.

The Need to Handle Matter in Treatment

The belief in matter will not disappear without the mental work that attacks and destroys it. Spiritual understanding disabuses the mind of material beliefs. This inner change is usually gradual. Slowly we let go of material pains and pleasures and the belief in matter, until we outgrow them entirely.

It is difficult to overcome matter, because mortal mind has constructed a very sophisticated and seemingly realistic form of material intelligence which seems to be "truth." But if any so-called knowledge conflicts with *Science and Health*, regardless of how logical and proven it may seem to be, time will prove it false. The advanced intelligence that Christ Jesus embodied was wholly spiritual.

As your work counteracts the belief in matter and material intelligence, you are freed of sickness, discord, age, lack, and limitation. Thus, the mental effort to break through the veil of matter is of great importance, and your success in this is measured in healing results.

Each time you challenge a material belief in consciousness, you weaken its hold. Some beliefs yield quickly. Others take many denials before they begin to break up and disappear.

Without this mental work, the belief in matter grows stronger and more tenacious. The longer we put off challenging and proving the unreality of matter the more difficult it is to overcome our belief in it. But with the treatment, you disabuse your mind of the illusion of matter and its false laws, and gain your freedom from the suffering it seems to cause.

In handling the belief in matter, you begin to disturb the hold animal magnetism has on you, and this sometimes causes a great deal of chemicalization. In challenging this lie, you bring your work out of theory into direct contact with the error in consciousness. By continuing to work, regardless of evil's resistance and reaction, you will realize victory over it. You can often feel a shifting within, as material beliefs yield to your work.

Handle matter as a totally subjective belief. It is an illusion in consciousness, and it can be broken down as you deny it through the synonyms. Think now — is there any life in matter? No. God is Life and the source of all being. Is there Truth or reality in matter? No. Divine Science never changes, while material knowledge always changes. It is always temporary and false. Is there Love in matter when it claims to cause suffering and death? No, never. Is there Mind, or intelligence, in lifeless, inanimate matter? No. Intelligence cannot create non-intelligence. Does Spirit, or substance, animate matter? No. Matter is inert and finite. Does matter represent Soul, or true identity? No. Divine laws never produce pain and suffering. Does it rest on the laws of divine Principle? No. All true being reflects Spirit, Mind, the one Principle, God. In this way, you reason about matter through the synonyms and slowly overcome it. You should research the terms matter, material law, cause and effect, etc., so that you have a thorough understanding of what you are denying.

2. MORTAL MIND

In addition to handling matter, you also need to go deeper into animal magnetism and analyze mortal mind in order to detect and destroy false traits that claim to be your mortal personality. In this part of the treatment, many negative emotions and false beliefs are uncovered in consciousness. You discern, one by one, traits within that need to be overcome.

Freeing consciousness of negative elements that claim to be your natural personality is very challenging. But once you have overcome a false belief or trait, you never have to handle it again. You are permanently healed of it by the fact that spiritual qualities unfold where a trait had been, and you cannot retrogress into a mortal state of mind that no longer seems real to you. In this way, you emerge gently out of the claim of mortality.

Separating the Mortal from the Immortal

You begin experiencing this inner renovation as you learn to separate mortal mind from immortal Mind. Both are entirely subjective. Mortal mind is invisible, intangible error. It is the opposite of immortal Mind, or true selfhood. Christian Science teaches how to detect and separate false thoughts and emotions from God-like qualities. If you are courageous and honest enough with yourself regarding sin or wrong thought-habits you are practicing, often ignorantly, this will be a major key to spiritualizing consciousness.

A study of God and man through the synonyms, reveals the divine nature of man. The traits and beliefs that claim to be your mortal selfhood are the opposite of man in God's likeness. Here again, you have two viewpoints — the mortal and the immortal. In your treatment, deny and reject mortal thoughts and emotions, and affirm the spiritual qualities. As you identify with this work, you will feel changes within followed by wonderful healings. If you are

76

experiencing some small change each day in how you think, then you are being successful in this work, outgrowing the old selfhood and putting on the new.

Detecting False Traits

Uncovering and overcoming mortal traits and emotions involves self-examination. There are many subtle, insidious and devious forms of mortal mind that we all harbor within without realizing that they are forms of sin. As a rule, we are not even aware that we are disobeying God, yet these traits obstruct our progress by shutting out the unfoldment of spiritual ideas. They are the antichrist resisting and negating the activity of the Christ in consciousness.

These false traits are forms of error that we have thought in for a lifetime. We live in them effortlessly, and identify with them as our personality. Many of these mental elements are so common that we do not think of them as wrong or sinful, until we begin to understand the true nature of man in Science. I will not overwhelm you with a long list of traits. Given here are some of the most common forms of animal magnetism that we need to detect and overcome:

Fear. We all have fear to overcome. There are those who are extremely fearful of many things. Fear is sin, because it disobeys the First Commandment by giving power and reality to evil. Search your thinking to see what you are afraid of, then overcome the fear by facing it down as mesmerism. Handle it in your treatment until it is no longer there, until you are not afraid.

Self-will: Self-will drives, forces, dominates. Self-will in some form — either dominating self-will or thwarted self-will — is the cause of almost every problem we have. Self-will is stubborn, self-righteous, rebellious, difficult, argumentative, antagonistic. One of the most subtle forms of animal magnetism is the use of self-will in the name of good — deciding on some good to be done, or determining what is best for others, and then forcing, driving, pressuring yourself or others to conform to these decisions. Self-will produces stress, discord, and conflict, and must be replaced with the humility that yields to God's will.

Criticism: A subtle form of hatred, habitual criticism finds fault with everything and everybody. Criticism is a subtle form of hatred. Too often, it is directed towards those nearest and dearest to us. It is a constant violation of the law of Love.

Materialism: The mesmerism of evil has a magnetic attraction that causes us to love worldly things rather than spiritual things. Worldliness is involvement with many human activities and obligations — the busy, busy life that has no time for God. We try to find comfort and satisfaction in a mortal life, rather than demonstrating spiritual understanding.

Personal sense: Through personal sense we cling to human beliefs, opinions, notions and prejudices with great self-righteousness. This mortal trait is preoccupied with what I think, I want, I believe, I know, etc. Personal sense does not listen to the "still, small voice" within because this closed mind rejects ideas that differ from its own views. Personal sense is easily hurt, quick to anger, sensitive, vindictive, resentful, antagonistic towards others when it believes they have said or done something to wrong, abuse, deceive, cheat, or hurt it. Personal sense resists the work of looking within, because the person doesn't want to face these faults and admit to any wrong thinking. Personal sense self-righteously defends mortal selfhood, and refuses to change.

The belief of being unwanted, unloved, rejected: If this seems to be what we experience, it is so because we have accepted an image of ourselves as being unworthy of love. We overcome this negative state of mind as we understand our true selfhood, and see that we are the beloved child of God.

The belief of inferiority: This claim includes self-pity, self-condemnation, guilt, timidity, extreme sensitiveness. Inferiority causes us to put off learning Science through a lack of confidence, and the fear of attempting new and unfamiliar experiences. Inferiority makes us believe that we are incapable of such demanding work.

The belief of being shut out of good: This produces heaviness, grief, sorrow, sadness. We cannot be shut out of good, for we are in the spiritual realm here and now. But if we rehearse all of the negative in human experience, with a sense of despair and hopelessness, how can we learn of this heavenly kingdom? We cannot have opposite views in the same mind at the same time.

Hatred: Hatred is the antichrist. We hate others because we believe they have wronged us through undeserved, unjust treatment, causing us to be unforgiving, revengeful, angry, hurt, bitter. Hatred may seem difficult to overcome because we feel justified in hating. Quite often these wrongs did happen to us, and we didn't deserve them. But there is no justification for hate. Hate violates the law of Love. We must forgive. We must love.

Pride: Pride and egotism are part of a belief of superiority, self-love and self-righteousness. One feels he has the right to look down on others as beneath him, and excluding and rejecting them. This belief in personal superiority lacks the humility that enables God to reach us. In God's sight, we are all equal.

Domination: This false trait exercises control over others from a self-righteous conviction that one knows what is best for them. Mentally manipulating, thwarting, or forcing another to be subservient, is excessive self-will. The claim of being dominated is just as wrong as dominating others. One is dominated through fear. A submissive individual suppresses his own ego or identity to make peace. It is just as wrong to be controlled by another's self-will as it is to be self-willed yourself.

There is often a tendency in the good person to be lovingly critical, lovingly self-righteous, lovingly dominating, and lovingly opinionated; or to be silently, secretly disapproving, angry, judgmental, or resentful. This is not being obedient to the law of Love.

This short list of mortal traits serves as an example of the sinful traits that need to be corrected. As you search your inner self for false traits, you will be able to handle them through study and prayer.

False Traits a Form of Sin

There is a great deal to the handling of mortal mind. Unless we take stock of our mental state and handle subtle forms of sin, we will have to overcome them through suffering.

Many false traits are so common that we do not even question them as being wrong or sinful, yet they are forms of sin that bring on very painful forms of mental and physical disease. In *The People's Idea of God*, Mrs. Eddy gives us a simple but profound thought: "We possess our own body, and make it harmonious or discordant according to the images that thought reflects upon it. The emancipation of our bodies from sickness will follow the mind's freedom from sin." A chronic problem is due to chronic wrong thinking, or sin. The problem will not heal until the mental disobedience has been corrected. Often the traits producing disease are so subtle and hidden that only through prayer in Christian Science can we discern and overcome them.

A research into the attributes of evil that are the opposite of the attributes of the synonyms, will furnish a good list of the mental elements to be handled.

Overcoming False Traits

The treatment rids consciousness of hidden traits and subtle forms of sin. Sometimes we have to work consciously for the uncovering and healing of a mortal trait. There are also times when the general treatment will uncover and destroy these errors without any special effort on our part. Some forms of animal magnetism dissolve and disappear without ever being clearly defined. Daily work can uncover and destroy false traits, so embedded in thinking and so much a part of consciousness that you are not aware of the need to correct them.

As you are healed of false traits, you become a better transparency for Truth. You replace hate with love, fear with confidence, pride and human opinion with humility, self-will with obedience to God. Thus you begin to actually live in your spiritual selfhood. The handling of mortal mind is all-important. You cannot pray often enough to be free from mortal traits.

Do keep in mind that the handling of mortal mind, like the handling of matter, must be done knowledgeably. To do this, we need to know what comprises mortal mind. What are the false beliefs and emotions that are to be overcome? How can we think in a more Godlike way? We have the ideal man revealed in Christian Science, but we must learn to *be* this man, to live up to the perfect concept.

Simply indulging in the analysis of mortal mind is not the purpose of this work. The reason for self-examination is to complete the uncovering by treating the error or sin as animal magnetism and casting it out. We must reform our thought-habits so as to reflect God's likeness. The treatment can accomplish this change or spiritualization of thought. When you detect and correct false traits, you are using the treatment as it was intended to be used — to spiritualize the whole of consciousness.

3. EVIL OR ANIMAL MAGNETISM

The spiritual universe and man are the effects of the one Mind, God. Material creation and mortal mind are the illusionary effects of animal magnetism. In order to have complete freedom from animal magnetism, we must look beyond the effects of animal magnetism, and handle the cause itself.

81

Christian Science is the most powerful form of intelligence on the earth, because with it, we can control and destroy all evil. In the fourth footstep of treatment, this spiritual intelligence is used to exercise our power over animal magnetism.

At this point, all of your affirmations of truth are brought directly to bear on animal magnetism. As truth in consciousness overcomes the belief in the power and reality of evil, evil must collapse. You bring your understanding of God into direct contact with evil, and wrestle with the source of all hypnotic suggestion. When you fearlessly use the truth to attack and wipe out the mesmerism of animal magnetism in your own consciousness, the healing effects of this mental battle are awesome. This is the most powerful part of your treatment. If you can control and destroy the mesmerism of evil subjectively, healing is inevitable. Sometimes it is instantaneous.

Mrs. Eddy has given us two facts about evil that give us dominion over it:

1. *Evil is not real. It is nothing. It does not exist.*
2. *Evil must be handled until it ceases its claim to have power or reality.*

We cannot handle evil as nothing by *assuming* that it is nothing. *We must prove this fact by demonstrating it.* Through the treatment, we argue against evil until we feel its hypnotic influence lessen and disappear. We can insist that it is nothing and resist it until it collapses into nothing. The healing results of this mental work are proof that evil is not real.

One main reason for failure in healing is an ignorance of how to handle animal magnetism. While evil is unreal, we cannot say it is nothing and ignore it. In mortal life, it appears to be a power greater than God. If we do not handle it, it handles us. Within our own mental sphere, we must face evil's hypnotic suggestions and resist them with the truth until we no longer feel or think them. We need to handle animal magnetism vehemently, persistently, fearlessly, until its hypnotic suggestions stop entering and controlling our thinking and healing is realized.

My booklet, *Animal Magnetism,* is a more thorough explanation of what evil is, how it operates, and how to handle it in Christian Science. I suggest you to read it in order to better understand this footstep of treatment.

Evil Analyzed

All discord and sin are the hypnotic work of evil accepted into consciousness. Evil is the hidden cause behind this mesmerism of matter and mortal mind. It can be defined as:

1. *A black, bitter hatred of Truth or the Christ-consciousness.*
2. *Sadism or the desire to cause pain and suffering.*
3. *Mental and physical cruelty.*

Evil is usually so offensive that we hesitate to handle it. We may be afraid to face it, for indeed it seems to be a powerful reality in human consciousness. But if we're going to be successful healers, we must be courageous enough to confront evil with the fact of its own unreality, and fight against it until we prove it to be nothing.

It is difficult to handle evil because of its resistance to being destroyed. Hypnotic suggestions are like tangible thoughts to consciousness. Their presence is felt mentally. When we start to handle evil, we find it resists our prayerful work. It will put us into a deep sleep, cause our minds to wander, make us think we do not need to do this work, bring interruptions, and even intensify the problem we are handling in order to make us think our work is not being effective.

Our prayerful work brings to light the aggressiveness with which evil resists its own destruction. Once we encounter such intense resistance, we begin to realize that, at this time and place in our work, evil cannot be casually dismissed as nothing. Its seeming ability to stop us from handling it, proves that it is far from nothing in human experience. We can be free of it only through a relentless mental battle with it in the heart of consciousness.

In fighting evil's resistance, we take control of our mind. We force the mesmeric beliefs within to weaken and give way, until they no longer claim to handle us. This is the destruction of animal magnetism.

Your realization of truth destroys the fear of evil. Loss of fear enables you to argue with total conviction against its seeming reality. *When fear is overcome, and you can stand absolutely unintimidated by evil's suggestions, you can no longer be influenced or controlled by it. Evil becomes nothing to you. It is the destruction of the fear of evil that enables you to handle it most successfully.* The loss of fear usually comes gradually as you are faithful to daily study and prayer.

Denying Evil

In the fourth footstep of treatment, you take the initiative against evil and insist silently or audibly that God is all and evil is nothing. You argue or fight *against* false beliefs and *for* the facts of Spirit in your own consciousness.

To deny evil correctly, you must first separate it from person, place or thing. This is all-important. You must see evil as impersonal suggestion. Then face matter, material law, mortal emotions and beliefs, and the basic elements of evil — its hatred of the Christ-consciousness, its sadism, its mental and physical cruelty.

Attack these forms of evil and vigorously argue against them. Confront animal magnetism with the fact of its own unreality. Denounce the power of evil. Become the attacker. Reach to the very source of evil's hidden forces and deny their presence and power. Argue with absolute authority that there is no law, energy, power or intelligence in animal magnetism; there is no evil cause or effect; there is no mind supporting evil, and no God in it. Then insist it is to stop arguing to you — it is to stop mesmerizing you!

Deny evil by using the synonyms for God. There is no life or being in evil, and no evil in Life; no truth or reality in evil, and no evil in Truth; no love or power in evil, and no evil in Love; no mind or intelligence in evil, and no evil in Mind; no spirit or substance in evil, and no evil in Spirit; no soul or ego in evil, and no evil in Soul; no principle or law in evil, and no evil in Principle.

Evil has only the illusions of its own lies, and these have no power over the Christ consciousness. Deny the mental energies of hate, sadism, and mental cruelty. Insist that animal magnetism cannot dominate, frustrate, thwart, or punish man.

Declare that evil has no foundation or source, no material man to act on or to act through. Insist that evil cannot think, feel or act. It has no material universe or physical man to afflict, for there is no matter. It never has influenced and never can influence you. It cannot deprive you of Christian Science by claiming to separate you from God. It cannot create a negative mental atmosphere that blinds you to your real selfhood. Deny that it can determine the events of your life or the structure and content of your mind. It cannot give you a mortal personality, or attach a mortal past to your being.

Attack evil with determination, vigor and directness, with absolute confidence in the power of Truth to overcome it. Never spare evil, or try to make your peace with it out of fear or apathy. It will use this weakness to further control your life. Reduce all discord to hypnotic suggestion and shut it out. *Refuse to think it!* Take possession of your mind and reject every false belief that claims to be there. Evil has no right to enslave consciousness with hypnotic beliefs. The more you prove this, the more you will be free of its influence.

This work can be designed to handle the general beliefs of mortal mind that seem chronic and universal, such as age, lack, material law, sickness, disease, heredity, mortality, and materialism. It can be used to overcome specific claims that seem to be manifesting themselves as personal problems.

When you realize that every form of discord and limitation is hypnotic suggestion coming from one cause, animal magnetism, your metaphysical work is greatly simplified. Instead of handling many different effects of evil, you can go straight to the cause — the seeming power and reality of evil — and handle that. When you deny evil's ability to reach you through hypnotic suggestion, when you argue vehemently against its power to mesmerize you until you lose your fear of it, then the cause is destroyed, evil collapses, and its harmful effects disappear.

It is encouraging to know that once hypnotic suggestions are thoroughly handled and destroyed, they cannot return. This purifying process is progressive. Your dominion over evil grows, and you are affected by it less and less as you challenge and overcome every form of mental control it tries to assume.

The fourth footstep is extremely powerful when it follows your affirmations of Truth in the previous footsteps. As you handle animal magnetism, you should feel the mesmerism give out and healing take place.

Handling Malicious Animal Magnetism

You should include in this footstep of treatment the handling of malicious animal magnetism in the form of the many 'isms' and 'ologies' in world thought. These have a harmful influence, and you must be alert to defend yourself against them. A list of these would include: black and white witchcraft, occultism, Roman Catholicism, communism, theosophy, oriental hypnosis, Hinduism, Satanism, spiritualism, atheism, agnosticism, numerology, astrology, humanism, hypnotism, psychology and *materia medica*. These specific forms of malicious animal magnetism should be handled frequently. There is an urgency to do this work, for this evil mental work is on the increase today.

Christian Science treatment is the one form of prayer that can protect you from malicious forms of hypnotism. A denial of all evil mental work in your treatment will not only protect you, but it will help free world consciousness of the scourge of secret hypnotic work.

Handling evil may seem complex and demanding, but it is not that difficult once you become experienced at doing this work. You can learn to do it and once you do, your healing work is scientific and certain, and powerful beyond anything you can imagine. Analyzing and handling evil is absolutely essential to spiritual healing. Mrs. Eddy states in *Science and Health*: "A knowledge of error and of its operations must precede that understanding of Truth which destroys error, until the entire mortal, material error finally disappears, and the eternal verity, man created by and of Spirit, is understood and recognized as the true likeness of his Maker."

Chapter X

FIFTH FOOTSTEP
THE ONENESS OF GOD AND MAN

In the fifth footstep, we affirm the oneness of God and man. We do not want to end our treatment with our thought focused on animal magnetism, in the negative part of treatment. So we lift thought up again into the affirmative part by realizing man's oneness with God.

In this footstep, we declare that God and man are one as cause and effect. As God's reflection, man is one with the divine Principle, Love. Since man is in the spiritual universe, and God is infinite and eternal, there is nowhere man can go to be outside of, or apart from, the one Father-Mother, God.

God causes, sustains, controls, and governs man's being. Mind is conscious of every detail that comprises a perfect life for man. The one Father not only meets man's every need, but He anticipates it, and provides the channel for fulfilling it. God gives all, and man has all that God gives. God never lets go of man, and we are that man. In reality, we can only know and have what God knows and has.

Being aware of this oneness with God is vital to our healing work. When we think of ourselves as mortals, separated from God, then our treatment usually becomes an abstract metaphysical exercise. But we are not far off from God; we are one with Him in the eternal now. As we exchange the material view for the spiritual, as we outgrow false images of sin, sickness, death, matter, evil, adversity, catastrophe and lack, and replace them with the true image of God and man as perfect cause and effect, we become increasingly aware that we are always one with God. When we are attuned to God, we move at one with Him.

Whatever the state of your present life, nevertheless your *true* being exists intact and undisturbed in God. It embodies indestructible good. Your true knowledge is divine Science, which you know, and you know you know. You are dearly loved by the one Father-Mother God. You are one with Mind's infinite reservoir of divine ideas. These constitute your true intelligence, wisdom, and understanding. Spirit is the substance of your being, and Soul is the source of your divine identity — your Christ-consciousness. You are governed by Principle, and so you reflect God's plan for you, unfolding in an orderly way.

Think about these statements, for you must begin identifying with the spiritual selfhood that is your real being. You are not one with material forces and mortal mind beliefs. You are one with the divine Mind. Whether you know it or not, this is so. You are man. As you de-mesmerize thought and lose your false views, you discover your true selfhood forever one with God.

This portion of treatment establishes your oneness with God as a present fact. If your denial of animal magnetism has been thorough and effective, the fifth footstep can be very inspiring. By affirming the truth and rising above the mesmerism of animal magnetism, you conclude the treatment in a spiritual state of mind.

SIXTH FOOTSTEP
PROTECT YOUR TREATMENT

The sixth footstep is very brief. In it, you once again protect your treatment by knowing that the treatment is a complete statement of Truth. Animal magnetism cannot annul or reverse its healing results. It is the Word of God and cannot return to you void. It must accomplish its purpose.

Chapter XI

GENERAL TREATMENT ILLUSTRATED

This chapter will illustrate how to give a general treatment. As I go through the six footsteps, remember that this is my version of the work and my interpretation of the synonyms. You should not accept my example as the only way to work, or think that you cannot deviate from this format. You must make the treatment yours, and adapt it to your own needs.

Each treatment is different. Sometimes you may find it difficult to begin the work, and so you may want to start off by vigorously handling animal magnetism. Sometimes the affirmations are especially inspiring. At other times the denial of animal magnetism is strong and clear. It is best to stay with that part of the work that it is so powerful, illuminating and helpful, and let the remaining footsteps wait until another day. Because the work is progressive, it is always changing, and that is why you need to be flexible in your approach to it.

My example of treatment will be a long one in order to illustrate how the work should be done. A thorough treatment usually takes at least an hour to complete. You should do this work for *yourself*, identifying with these statements of Truth, and thinking them through carefully.

First Footstep: Protect your Treatment

Begin by protecting your treatment. Grow quiet and in the stillness of thought, declare: This is a Christian Science treatment.

It is the Word of God, and the truth about God and man. This treatment cannot be annulled or reversed by animal magnetism. No malicious mental malpractice or world belief can cause this work to be null and void. Christian Science was discovered and founded by Mary Baker Eddy. It is the promised Comforter. It is the Science of Christianity, based on the teachings of Christ Jesus, our Way-shower.

This first footstep is short and simple. But if you want to add a stronger declaration at this time, you should do so. Your circumstances may be such that you need to be very protective of your work. If so, then you should be quite insistent that animal magnetism cannot keep you from giving a healing treatment.

Second Footstep: Declaring God through the Synonyms

In the second footstep, define God by relating the synonyms to each other. Begin this footstep with one of Mrs. Eddy's definitions for God: "GOD The great I AM, the all-knowing, all-seeing, all-acting, all-wise, all-loving, and eternal; Principle; Mind; Soul; Spirit; Life; Truth; Love; all substance; intelligence."

Next, take the synonyms in whatever order you care to, and relate them to each other. When you begin your treatment with a different synonym each day, this gives inspiration and variety to your work and keeps it from becoming stale and routine. You might begin by relating Life to the other synonyms.

Life is being. It is the ever-presence of God creating and maintaining all things in perfect harmony. Man and the universe are eternal because Life is eternal — without beginning or end. Life is health, vitality, strength, freedom, boundless bliss. There is no opposing thought-force in reality to obstruct the activity of Life and so all manifestation of Life lives effortlessly as the unfoldment of God's being. Life is harmony and perfection unfolding in the eternal now.

Life is Truth, reality. Life is ever-conscious of Truth or divine reality; therefore Life is immutable and immortal, because

Truth is immutable and immortal. Divine Life never wanes, never wears out, is never tired, because Truth, the foundation of being, is eternal. Life, indestructible being, is an eternal verity. Life alone is real. Life and Truth maintain honesty, integrity, justice, and mercy in man and the universe. The attributes of Life — joy, activity, bliss, freedom, immortality — represent true being or reality.

Life is Love. All being is the expression of Love. Life is permeated with divine Love. In the spiritual realm, Love is the only presence and power, and so Life is lived in the atmosphere of divine Love. Life is harmonious in its unfoldment, because it is governed by the law of Love, in which all ideas relate to each other through Love. Love's ideas express perfect unity in the unfoldment of eternal Life. Its ideas rejoice in the freedom and boundless bliss of spiritual Life, and live to love, for Love is a law of Life.

Life is Mind. Life expresses divine intelligence. All there is to be, God is; all there is to know, God knows; and so being is the expression of perfect intelligence. This intelligence manifests itself as spiritual ideas, creative ideas, intelligent ideas, practical ideas. Life is one with Mind's infinite reservoir of ideas, which is the life-giving source of all intelligence. Each living thing is an idea of Mind, expressing the harmony and perfection of the divine intelligence that creates and sustains it. The spiritual understanding which illumines Mind is eternal; therefore Life is eternal, for there is nothing in Mind to oppose or obstruct Life.

Life is Spirit. The substance of Life is spiritual. The divine energies of Spirit create all outline, form, and color, and these visible manifestations of Spirit are the body of God, the perfect expression of His being. The forms which express Life originate in Spirit, and are indestructible, perfect, intelligent, benign, pure, loving and good. Divine Life and spiritual cause and effect are one. Life is ever-conscious of the spiritual source of all things. Spirit is the only cause and creator, and this spiritual cause expresses eternal life in the spiritual universe and man,

Life is Soul. Soul gives to living things identity and individuality. Life images forth the qualities of Soul — loveliness, grace, beauty, harmony and perfection. Each idea is an individual expression of the inexhaustible resources of Soul, and is always one with the spiritual source that creates it. The spiritual senses see and hear the universe as God has made it, complete in its spiritual wholeness; and Life is lived in the harmony and perfection of this Soul-like atmosphere.

Life is Principle. Life is governed by the laws of God. All being moves at one with God, under the direction and control of the divine Principle, Love. The laws governing Life are loving, intelligent, spiritual and scientific. Life expresses order, plan, and unity. All expressions of Life exist as part of God's plan. As perfect ideas, they are unified by the laws of Principle, move in accord with it, and are held forever in place by it. Life can never exist apart from the divine laws that govern throughout eternity.

As you relate Life to each of the synonyms, think what each statement means. Visualize it. Accept it as the right viewpoint.

For a thorough treatment, you should also relate the remaining synonyms to each other.

You can relate Truth to the other five synonyms.

Truth is reality. Truth is the one true Science that reveals man as the divine idea, made in God's likeness. Because Truth is eternal, immutable, immortal, creation is eternal, immutable, immortal. Creation has a spiritual dimension and Truth reveals its structure and content. Truth is expressed in the integrity, honesty, faithfulness, justice and mercy of God as He cares for man.

Truth is Love. It is a scientific fact that divine Love is the only power. God governs creation with divine Love, for the one true cause of all things real is a harmless, affectionate thought-force. Reality is radiant with Love, and all scientific knowledge is aglow with the inspiration of Love. Love is the reality of being. Reality is filled with Love manifested in an infinity of spiritual and scientific ideas.

Truth is Mind. The intelligence, wisdom, and understanding of divine Mind are infallible because they are Truth. An understanding of Truth is reality. Mind knows all Truth, or divine Science. Only the ideas of Mind, expressing divine intelligence, are Truth. Truth reveals all that can be known about Mind and its spiritual creation — man and the universe.

Truth is Spirit. Reality is Spirit, divine substance, all good; and all things real have only the substance of Spirit. The spiritual dimension is divine substance, or God's thoughts. Truth reveals that all substance, all that comprises the universe and man, is spiritual in origin. All things are created, governed and maintained by Spirit, and so reality is spiritual cause and effect.

Truth is Soul. Truth is one with Soul's creativity or originality, which is governed by laws of divine Science. The divine identity of each idea reflects Truth alone. Soul's spontaneity and inspiration are always imparting to its ideas the truth of being, therefore Truth, or the Christ-consciousness, is the only identity known to man. Truth, aglow with Love, is Soul, and imparts honesty, integrity, and justice to man.

Truth is Principle, law. The spiritual, moral, and scientific laws of God are the foundation of reality. Truth unfolds the scientific nature of the spiritual realm, and defines the spiritual laws, the divine plan, order, and unity underlying all that is real. Truth and Principle are one because they are both immutable, immortal. Reality is created and governed by Principle. All that is known as Truth must conform to the laws of God, and manifest the divine Principle, Love.

Next you can relate Love to the four remaining synonyms.

Love is power, relationship. Love is the presence of joy, happiness, and peace. It motivates and permeates all that God does. In God's universe, all ideas unfold through the effortless action of Love. Love is the only power in reality. It draws all ideas together in perfect harmony, and blesses creation with infinite good.

Love is Mind. Love is relationship, and the only intelligent relationship is a loving one. Therefore, all true relationships are bound together in pure affection. They express divine intelligence, and unfold in the unified plan of divine Love. The power of Love is irresistible because it expresses divine wisdom and understanding. Mind radiates Love in all that it unfolds, and Mind cares for all that it creates. The intelligence of Mind is permeated with Love, and the action of Mind is motivated by Love. The intelligence, wisdom, and understanding of Mind and the gentleness, warmth, and goodness of Love are one.

Love is Spirit. Love is the substance of being. The spiritual forces creating and governing all things are Love. The spiritual dimension is permeated with divine Love, and so substance is harmless because Love is harmless. Spiritual being is governed by infinite Love, and Love is expressed in forms that are indestructible and eternal.

Love is Soul. Soul and Love are one; and each manifestation of Soul, embodying its own individuality, expresses Love. Love's joy, inspiration, warmth, beauty, and graciousness are the very essence of Soul. The loveliness of Love is Soul expressed in individual identity. The creations of Soul unfold and ripen into fruition as they are born in the atmosphere of Love and nurtured by it.

Love is Principle. Love is a spiritual law, a divinely intelligent law. This law exercises its power within and without all things. It governs the order, plan and unity unfolding from Principle by binding all things together in the oneness of Love. All cause is Love, the only power and presence in reality. Love enforces the laws of

Principle with divine wisdom and understanding, and so unifies all things in perfect harmony.

Next you can relate Mind to the remaining synonyms.

Mind is intelligence. All that can be known is included in divine intelligence, infallible wisdom, and spiritual understanding. The pure intelligence of Mind creates and cares for man and the universe. The Science of being is made known to man through divine ideas that give to him infallible intelligence, supreme wisdom, and spiritual understanding.

Mind is Spirit. The substance of reality is the manifestation of divine intelligence. Mind's ideas have the substance of Spirit, the substance of Life, Truth, and Love. Therefore, they are eternal, unchanging, infinite. Mind's reservoir of ideas is spiritual in nature, and Mind works only through spiritual cause and effect. It unfolds perfect and harmonious ideas. The real cause that gives outline, substance, and color to the universe and man is Mind. Mind, being spiritual, is intelligent, harmless, and good. It blesses and perpetuates all that it creates.

Mind is Soul. The intelligent activity of Mind is expressed in the creativity of Soul. The ideas of Mind unfold in beauty and originality. All true identity has the grace and comeliness of Soul, and the intelligence and wisdom of Mind. The ideas of Mind are the individuality of man. These ideas are not only intelligent, wise and good, but they also express beauty, originality, harmony, and perfection.

Mind is Principle. The ideas of Mind operate in accord with Principle and its laws. Man and the universe are the intelligent expression of Mind. They unfold in an orderly way, and Mind maintains plan, purpose and unity in them through divine laws. The ideas of Mind are one with Principle, and unfold according to God's plan and purpose for them. In the whole of creation there is one Principle, Mind, one supreme, intelligent cause expressing itself in one perfect effect governed by divine laws.

Next you can relate Spirit to Soul and Principle.

Spirit is substance. Underlying all things is the spiritual dimension wherein rests the cause and continuity of reality. The scientific facts of reality are spiritual, and express Life, Truth, Love. Thus the substance of all things is Spirit. Only as man and the universe are interpreted spiritually can they be understood.

Spirit is Soul. Divine substance is manifested in infinite individuality. The spiritual ideas of Mind are given identity through Soul. These ideas, expressed in and as the universe and man, are imbued with the qualities of Soul — individuality, beauty, grace, harmony, and perfection. Soul has only the substance of Spirit, God. The qualities of Soul are spiritual in nature, and so the ideas of Soul are true substance. All ego, or identity, is filled with spiritual understanding, true knowledge, perfect intelligence, pure love — individualized as true substance or being.

Spirit is Principle. The only Principle underlying all things is spiritual. Divine law, plan and purpose are real substance, for these alone endure. The substance of Spirit is governed by the law of Life, the law of Love, the law of intelligence. Spiritual cause is one with the laws of Principle, and expresses only those ideas that are obedient to Principle. The substance of the universe is indestructible, harmless, good, because it is created and governed by the divine Principle, Love. Spiritual laws govern all that God creates in perfect unity — one divine cause and effect, perfect God, perfect man, perfect universe.

Now relate Soul to Principle.

Soul is identity, individuality, ego; Principle is law, order, plan, unity. Soul is Principle. True identity is governed by the laws of Principle, and is obedient to them. Every idea in Mind is subject to the divine Principle, Love, which creates and governs it. God expresses Himself in creativity, and all that He makes reflects divine plan and purpose. Each manifestation of Soul is unique, individual, original, because individuality is a divine law, which impels Soul to give each thing its own identity. Soul cannot repeat itself. Soul never violates the absolute laws of Principle in its creativity, and so all that it creates has plan and purpose in God's universe. The laws of Principle govern the ideas of Soul by giving them an intelligent and stable foundation. In the spiritual realm, the unfoldment of all identity is ordered, planned, and directed by the divine Principle, Love.

You can conclude this footstep by considering the whole of God as the one cause and creator, the only Father and Mother, All-in-all. He is ever-present, caring for all, enfolding His ideas in infinite good. Sometimes in this second footstep, it is good simply to consider God as a whole, and ponder each synonym as it relates to the nature of God, the great I AM.

By relating the synonyms to each other, each treatment should unfold new ideas about God and man. In this example, there is much I have not touched upon concerning the synonyms. But it will serve as a guide for your own metaphysical work.

Sometimes this part of the treatment will be so inspiring that it brings a flow of ideas. When this happens, you should stay with the second footstep, for it is the realization of Truth that spiritualizes thought and heals. At such times, the entire daily treatment can be devoted to this one footstep.

The second footstep is focused on God alone. Through these affirmations of Truth, you are developing the spiritual viewpoint, disciplining yourself to think in spiritual facts. The treatment is forever bringing new approaches to your affirmations and denials. It is never stereotyped, never a formula. No two treatments are alike. Your work should become spontaneous, a daily communication with God through which His thoughts become yours, and you find your oneness with Him.

When you are handling specific problems such as sickness, false traits, age, lack, discord, limitation, this positive part of treatment can emphasize health, true identity, eternal life, abundance, harmony, infinite good. It can be adapted to meet each need as it arises.

The purpose of this work is not to rehearse statements of Truth, but to become accustomed to *thinking in spiritual ideas*, so that you have a mental atmosphere through which God can reach you.

Third Footstep: Affirming Man and the Universe Through the Synonyms

In the third footstep, we relate man and the universe to the synonyms. Remember that this work is mainly for *yourself*, to spiritualize your own consciousness. Identify with it. When you declare man, you are discovering your true identity. What is the truth about man, about you? It is found in the synonyms.

Man expresses Life, being. Man exists as a complete and perfect idea of God. Perfection is natural to his being. Since man is the effect of the one divine cause, nothing can sever his relationship with the Father. Because God is indestructible, man is indestructible. Man is never outside of divine Life. He lives in Life. He expresses eternal Life, and possesses every good thing. Man is deathless, eternal. His real being is held intact forever in the one Life. Only what God is doing for man ever comes into his experience. As God's reflection, he expresses health, vitality, activity, freedom, joy and happiness.

Man knows Truth as reality. Truth is the intelligence of man. Man reflects the Science known to God, and Truth alone is real to him. Man thinks in Truth effortlessly, for it is the whole of his being. He knows the Truth, and he knows he knows it. Truth or Science is practical and rational to him. Truth is all to him and there is nothing beyond it. Nothing is unknown to God, or to man in His likeness. With a consciousness filled with Truth, nothing unlike Truth

99

can enter his being. As God's child he expresses honesty, reliability, trustworthiness, justice and mercy — all that represents Truth.

In the realm of Love, man is the beloved. He is secure in divine Love. As God's idea, he is as safe as God Himself. Nothing can cloud over his sense of oneness or unity with the divine Principle, Love. As the child of God, man expresses the qualities of Love — affection, kindness, tenderness, gentleness, patience, compassion, forgiveness, humility, and gratitude. These qualities enable man to reflect the power of Love. In the whole of man's being there is not one harmful mental or physical element. Man knows and expresses only the purity of divine Love.

Man dwells in the eternal Mind. As the reflection of Mind, man does not believe; he knows. Mind knows all things, and man's reflection of this knowing is perfect, complete. Being one with Mind, man receives only the mental impressions of God, good. He is the work of God, obedient to Mind alone. In humility, he discerns and reflects the spiritual ideas that unfold as his very being. These ideas are manifested as intelligence, wisdom, and understanding. They are used by man in all that he thinks and says and does. These ideas, spiritual, creative, intelligent, practical, meet his every need.

The substance of man's existence is Spirit, the origin of life, and so his spiritual existence is good, healthful, holy. Man understands the nature of the spiritual dimension. He knows he is never outside its presence. Man lives in true substance, for spiritual qualities and ideas are the substance of his being. His senses can discern only the spiritual nature of all things, for he lives as the expression of God, Spirit.

Man expresses Soul. Man's ego or identity is wholly spiritual. His true individuality is "hid with Christ in God." Divine ideas unfold to maintain his perfect reflection of God. His ego is creative, loving, gracious, inspired, beautiful, Godlike, poised in the realm of Love. Through Soul, man has individualized in consciousness a perfect selfhood. He is the expression of the pure and sinless qualities of Soul, and lives in the uncontaminated realm of Mind. He is complete in Soul.

The laws of Principle govern man. These laws give unity and plan to his life. He reflects the law of Love, the law of Life, the law of intelligence, the law of abundance. God created a universe to bless man, and he lives in a totally benign environment. His life unfolds according to the laws of Principle. Obedient to these laws, man is blessed with dominion over all the earth.

When you have related man to the synonyms, declare, "I am that man!" Realize that these statements are the truth about you. They tell you who you really are. The more clearly you discern God's nature, and man's nature as His reflection, the more these facts govern your entire being. Identify with your statements about man.

As part of the third footstep, you should apply the synonyms to your image of the universe. To do this, affirm the facts about the universe as you did about man. What do the synonyms tell you about creation?

The universe, like man, is spiritual. Underlying the forms and forces of creation is the spiritual dimension. This dimension, or reality, has a definite structure and content, scientifically revealed in Christian Science.

In this realm divine Life creates and sustains the existence of all living things through inexhaustible resources. Life fills all time and space. In the whole of God's universe there is not one place where divine Life does not exist as God's presence as a pulsating, thinking cause.

Truth declares throughout all of creation the spiritual and scientific facts about the universe. The universe rests upon a foundation of scientific, moral, and spiritual laws. The spiritual realm is reality. The fact about reality is that it is a manifestation of harmony and perfection emanating from eternal Truth.

The universe is an expression of Love. It is wholly benign, harmless, and good. Every atom is controlled by divine intelligence and love. Not one atom can act apart from divine Love, and so all atomic structure is good, and all atomic behavior is kind, gentle, harmonious, for Love is All-in-all.

Creation manifests pure intelligence. Its origin is in Mind. Mind unfolds itself in an infinity of ideas, each perfect in itself, each part of a perfect whole. God creates and governs the universe through supreme wisdom and intelligence; therefore the laws and energies that control atomic action are the divinely intelligent thoughts of God. All things real have a spiritual origin in Mind.

Spirit is the substance of the universe. Mind inhabits the spiritual dimension as the final cause of creation. It is a thinking cause, a spiritual power of intelligence and love. All that is real originates in divine intelligence, in the substance of Spirit. All atomic form and action are one with this spiritual cause. Thus, all that exists is under the gentle power, control and care of Spirit, God.

The universe is a manifestation of Soul. The beauty, harmony, and perfection of the universe and nature must have a source or cause. Soul is the creative Mind that gives to each thing its own unique individuality or identity. Soul forms and colors each idea, and blends together these ideas into a perfect whole. The universe   expresses the beauty of holiness, the creativity of Soul.

The spiritual universe is obedient to the laws of divine Principle. The laws governing creation are intelligent and loving. These laws give unity, plan, and direction to the unfoldment or evolution of the universe. Because the divine Principle, Love, is the lawgiver to all things, the whole of creation is harmless, benign, good.

This is an example of how the synonyms enable you to develop a spiritual viewpoint of the universe.

The second and third footsteps are the affirmative part of treatment. The statements are all positive. What you are trying to do is realize the Truth, and so replace the material view with the spiritual. All of the statements in this portion of the work should be positive declarations of Truth, without a denial of animal magnetism. It does require practice to discipline yourself to think in spiritual realities alone. But if you persist, it becomes natural to think in the right viewpoint.

Fourth Footstep: The Denial of Animal Magnetism

In the first three footsteps, the declarations of Truth are made in a positive, receptive state of mind; but the denial of animal magnetism is made with strong, even vehement, rejections of evil. You are working to de-mesmerize consciousness, to free it of every claim of animal magnetism.

To do this, you can begin by denying matter through the synonyms. Declare that there is no life in matter, and no matter in Life or being; no truth in matter, and no matter in Truth or reality; no love or power in matter, and no matter in Love; no mind in matter, and no matter in Mind or intelligence; no spirit in matter, and no matter in Spirit or substance; no soul in matter, and no matter in Soul or true identity; no law or principle in matter, and no matter in divine Principle and its laws.

As you go through the denial of matter each day, think what these powerful statements mean. Declare them with careful concentration, and with conviction. In doing this, you begin to free your mind of the belief in matter and its seeming laws.

Next you can declare against the false traits of mortal mind by stating that there is no fear, hatred, or self-will in man. There are no subtle forms of sin, such as criticism, self-righteousness, self-justification, self-love, anger, impatience, irritation, disappointment, guilt, self-condemnation. Determine what false traits are most predominant in yourself, and with careful reasoning see through these self-hypnotic states. Deny that they are any part of your being.

103

Let's take fear, for example. Declare with strong conviction that there is no law, energy, power, or intelligence in fear. If God is All-in-all, and man and the universe reflect His love and intelligence, what is there to be afraid of? Is there anything outside of God to fear? No. Is there anything in God to fear? No. Then face the things you seem to fear — the future, a discordant relationship, lack, sickness, etc., and see that your fear is hypnotic suggestion arguing that God is not All-in-all. Resist the fear and the mortal, material beliefs that are causing the fear, until they disappear from consciousness.

How would you handle criticism? This is a subtle form of hatred that defies the law of Love. So reason on this. See it as a common form of animal magnetism so universal that everyone criticizes without considering it to be a hypnotic state through which animal magnetism claims to control the mind. Is there Love in criticism? Does it give Life? Is it divinely intelligent? Is it principled? Is there any Truth in criticism? Is it part of Soul, or one's divine identity? No! Then it does not originate in God. Therefore, you can argue that it is no part of man. In the whole of God's universe there is not one critical thought — not one! Think about that. Then know that you cannot be mesmerized into breaking the law of Love by thinking or speaking critical thoughts. You cannot be made to fear criticism. It is important to deal directly with this belief and handle it in treatment, if you are to be free of it.

As a rule, these false traits do not dissolve immediately, but they do yield gradually to your daily work. Force them to yield by resisting them in the name of God. Demand that they loose you and let you go!

I urge you to handle self-will daily. At the bottom of almost every problem we have, there is either thwarted or aggressive self-will. Know that animal magnetism cannot make you resist the need to do this mental work through the claim of willfulness, stubbornness, human opinion, resentment, human outlining, self-righteousness, self-justification, self-love. There are countless forms of self-will to be uncovered and destroyed. Self-will is never overcome completely with a few treatments. This is a long-term demonstration, for self-will comes in so many subtle ways..

In this part of your treatment, deny every mortal trait that claims to be part of your being. If you do, you will feel these beliefs loosening in consciousness and disappearing. Then gradually the elements of your spiritual selfhood will unfold to replace them. This is true reformation.

What you are doing here is handling subtle forms of sin. In the previous footstep, you claimed the true nature of man as loving, honest, intelligent, pure, wise and good. Now you must deny the false nature of man. Insist that animal magnetism cannot handle you through mortal mind traits that are ungodlike. One by one, deny that there is any life, power, or reality in guilt, or self-justification, or anger. As you uncover these negative emotions in yourself, erase them. You can and should let this part of treatment unfold; otherwise you may become overwhelmed by seeing so much error in yourself. But do consider the need for self-examination. Uncovering and handling false traits bring about tremendous healing. It reforms and purifies your thinking.

Argue vehemently against such claims as depression, nervousness, guilt, resentment, revenge, hatred. Handle sensualism, materialism, a negative or hostile state of mind. We each have our own mortal disposition with its combination of beliefs. By recognizing and denying those that seem to be your mortal personality, you will experience a great change in yourself.

You can handle these claims and overcome them because they have never been part of your real being. Once you realize that they are not a permanent part of consciousness, you begin to separate yourself from them. You see how the belief and believer are one; and they are no part of your real being. God supports your resistance to sin; and once seen as the antichrist, wrong thoughts practically destroy themselves. Your work is to bring the Christ-consciousness into contact with erroneous thought-habits, and side with the Christ in overcoming them.

In handling matter and mortal mind, you handle the effects of animal magnetism. But you need to go one step further and handle the cause itself. In this, you must be strong, even vehement, in your denial. Force animal magnetism out of consciousness. Fight with it! Look through every kind of mortal belief, and see behind it evil arguing to you. Then face the evil and declare: There is no power, law, intelligence, or energy in you. There is no Principle or law in you; no Soul or ego in you; no Spirit or substance in you; no Mind, intelligence, or wisdom in you; no Love or power in you; no Truth or reality in you; no Life or being in you. Therefore, you are to stop arguing to me! You are to stop mesmerizing me! You are to loose me and let me go!

Deny specific suggestions. Declare to animal magnetism, You cannot make me afraid. You cannot make me lack. You cannot make me sick, or handle my mind in any way. Stand up to evil! Back it down again and again. Reject its hypnotic suggestions. Refuse to think anything evil or discordant. You must grapple with it, as Jacob did, until you have dominion over it.

Find your own way of resisting evil, but do it! Don't neglect this part of treatment. If your affirmations of Truth have been strong and inspiring, this vehement denial of evil will so challenge it that it will weaken and dissolve and vanish from thought. *This is often the moment in your treatment when affirmation of Truth and denial of evil bring about the most powerful results.*

Take control of your mind and resist animal magnetism with the absolute conviction that good destroys evil. Each time you declare the simple facts — that evil has no law, energy, intelligence or power, no reality or substance, that there is no Mind in evil and no God in it — you are exercising your dominion over it.

In this part of treatment, deny specific problems that you are trying to overcome, reducing them to mesmeric suggestions and handling them as such. This enables you to stop believing in them as real. If you are giving a general treatment, you may not always need to deny specific claims. But you can deny beliefs of heredity, birth, age, death, and other universal claims.

It is also good to deny forms of malicious animal magnetism that claim to work against Christian Science treatment. Declare that there is no malicious malpractice, Roman Catholicism, communism, occultism, orientalism, witchcraft, Satanism, astrology, numerology, psychology, etc. There is no 'ism' or 'ology' named or unnamed, known or unknown, that can harm or influence you, or claim to paralyze or obstruct the power of the Christ-consciousness. As you progress in Christian Science and understand the seeming power of these mental forces, it will become clear how essential it is to do this protective work for yourself daily.

While you must handle animal magnetism, the fourth foot step should not, as a rule, overshadow the rest of the treatment. The denial of evil must be done; but it is the realization of Truth that heals.

This fourth footstep covers three basic points: the handling of matter and material beliefs; the handling of mortal mind; and then the strong denial of animal magnetism. In handling a specific problem, determine the cause. Whatever the discord or error may seem to be, its origin is in evil's hatred of the Christ-consciousness, its sadism, its mental and physical cruelty. Fight it out with the cause — animal magnetism. When you have been successful in this battle by destroying some hypnotic hold of evil, you will know it, for you are mentally free of the suggestion and healing follows.

You must take the time to do a thorough job of the denial portion of treatment, for this brings continuous healing and unfoldment; whereas when you ignore animal magnetism and confine the work to positive declarations of Truth alone, the work may fail to bring about healing results.

Take up mental arms against every belief of animal magnetism and force it out of consciousness. There may be times when almost the entire treatment is given to the denial of animal magnetism. The work should be adapted to each day's needs. As a rule, the affirmation of Truth is so important that it should have the major portion of time given to treatment. But there are exceptions to this. When error is stirred, or aggressive, or coming to the surface of consciousness to be destroyed, then you need to recognize this and devote sufficient work to destroying it. The approach to treatment changes daily. If you feel the need to devote time to the denial of evil and it is proving effective, then stay with it.

In this fourth footstep, bring the truth to bear on false suggestions and argue against them until they weaken and give out. When some form of animal magnetism is especially stubborn, you usually have to wear it down by a relentless denial of its seeming reality or existence. This repetitious denial of evil can go on for days, even weeks, in order to counteract the hypnotic state and destroy it. *But you can do this!* Do make full use of the healing power in this part of your treatment.

The Fifth and Sixth Footsteps of Treatment

In the fifth footstep, affirm the oneness of God and man. Declare that God is the one Father-Mother, and man is His child. God and man are one as cause and effect. This is true right here, right now. While we may seem to be separated from God, He knows we are not separated from Him. He never lets go of us. Man is always one with Him, under His care, enveloped in His love. Man is under the influence of Mind alone, and one with divine intelligence, and you are that man.

Work with this fifth footstep until thought is one with God, and you are inspired with a spiritual sense that is joyous, positive, loving, peaceful and good.

Then again, in the sixth footstep, protect your work by knowing that this treatment is the Word of God and cannot be annulled or reversed. It will not return void, but must accomplish its purpose. In the words of Isaiah, "So shall my word be that goeth forth out of my mouth: it shall not return unto me void, but it shall accomplish that which I please, and it shall prosper in the thing whereto I sent it."

This example covers a general treatment. It takes at least an hour to go through all six footsteps. In the beginning of your work, you may find it difficult, if not impossible, to focus for an hour on the treatment. Such thinking is not a state of mind that we are accustomed to. You will also encounter the intense resistance of animal magnetism to being uncovered and destroyed. This re-sistance, coupled with the work of learning a new method of thinking, poses one of the greatest challenges imaginable.

If you find the work difficult, take comfort in the fact that everyone who takes up this work finds it a great challenge in the beginning. So do not be discouraged if you have to struggle when giving your first treatments. If you find you can only concentrate on the work for a few minutes, then try doing the treatment in seg-ments throughout the day. Begin in the morning with what you can manage to do. Then whenever you can find the time, sit down and take up the work where you left off. Continue this during the day and into the evening until you complete the six footsteps.

With such determination, you will wear down the resis-tance of animal magnetism and begin giving the entire treatment at one time. Again, I assure you that this struggle to master the treat-ment is not unusual. I have never known anyone to undertake the treatment, and begin immediately doing an hour's metaphysical work. So you are not alone if you find the work difficult.

In the beginning of this work, you could try doing a simplified version of the six footsteps. You might begin by briefly protecting your treatment, and then relating one synonym to the other six — perhaps one that you are studying at the time. Next, relate man and the universe to that one synonym. In the fourth footstep deny matter and the basic mortal traits — fear, hatred, and self-will. Then specifically deny animal magnetism as a cause, power, law or energy claiming to be a power apart from God. Then reaffirm the oneness of God and man, and protect your treatment.

This shorter version is one that you can think through from beginning to end in less time. Being shorter, you can finish it. It is my opinion that it is better to give a short but complete treatment, rather than go over and over the first and second footsteps each time you try to give a treatment without getting beyond that point. There is a good feeling about completing all six footsteps.

You need to concentrate intensely on every declaration of truth and denial of error you make. Think about the work you are doing. Focus as hard as you can on the ideas you are working with. As you do, you break down the resistance of animal magnetism to your work and your treatment is then a constant source of joy and inspiration. And it heals!

Chapter XII

THE PURPOSE AND POWER
OF A GENERAL TREATMENT

The treatment is simple, but very effective. There are no insignificant parts to it. The second and third footsteps bring to consciousness the spiritual view; the fourth footstep forces out the material view; and the fifth footstep reinforces the spiritual view again. The power of this prayerful work has barely been tapped.

Too often Christian Science is used to overcome an urgent problem — sickness, a misunderstanding, a challenge in business, etc. But when the claim is met, study and treatment are usually shelved until the individual is forced to meet another challenge. An occasional demonstration of it may be adequate in handling lesser problems; but overcoming the belief of age, chronic lack, traits of character, so-called incurable disease — indeed, the whole of mortal existence — requires dedicated and consistent work.

In the textbook, Mrs. Eddy writes, "The infinite Truth of the Christ-cure has come to this age through a 'still, small voice,' through silent utterances and divine anointing which quicken and increase the beneficial effects of Christianity. I long to see the consummation of my hope, namely, the student's higher attainments in this line of light." Your work with treatment is your own demonstration of these "higher attainments." You are striving to demonstrate more than comfort in a material sense of life. The goal is to achieve the state of spiritual consciousness that will enable you to heal as Christ Jesus and Mrs. Eddy did. You are working to understand God as they did.

The Three Levels of Consciousness

A general treatment goes beneath the surface of the mind and affects all levels of consciousness. To illustrate this point, visualize the mind as having three levels: the outer level, the middle level, and the innermost level. The outer level represents the visible manifestation of our thinking through which we make contact with the world, and express our thoughts and feelings. The second level is a mixture of Godlike qualities, and mortal beliefs that comprise the human personality. This level remains predominately mortal throughout our lifetime unless we change it through spiritualizing consciousness. The innermost thoughts of the third level hold our basic philosophy or viewpoint of man and the universe.

If our philosophical viewpoint is mainly materialistic, if we believe that the universe and man are actually caused and governed by the mindless forces of matter, then the inner level is very dark. This darkness affects the middle level of consciousness, making the personality materialistic. It embodies fear, selfishness, and hatred — personal sense in all of its many aspects. This mortal personality then objectifies itself in a mortal life. It continually produces sickness, discord, lack, and limitation in the outer experience.

There is usually very little change in our human experience until there has been definite change in the inner levels of the mind. Such change comes as this inner self is spiritualized by Truth active in consciousness.

When we work in the general treatment, we are able to treat this innermost level and change it from the material viewpoint to the spiritual, for this treatment reaches into the inner core of the mind and actually changes an entrenched material philosophy. When we realize some atom of truth and destroy some claim of animal magnetism in this inner level, then this change affects the upper levels of consciousness. Once you realize, for example, the law of

112

Love as the Principle of being, you are compelled to correct hatred, criticism, and fear. You then express love and forgiveness naturally. As you discern Mind and its ideas as ever-present, you come to trust and rely upon these ideas to guide and protect you; you have more wisdom and intelligence; you express more confidence and success. Spiritual unfoldment deep in consciousness affects your disposition in many ways, and then is manifested outwardly in a better life.

Inner Change through Treatment

The materialistic philosophy embedded in the innermost level of consciousness is slow to change because it is entrenched within as solid conviction. It is a false structure of intelligence that you have thought in for a lifetime. Through your prayerful work, you can change this basic philosophy. Thought is never so hardened that it cannot change. Even the most deeply rooted material belief eventually softens and yields to proper metaphysical work. No error is forever impervious to the prayer of affirmation and denial.

The general treatment is very effective in overcoming the seeming cause or source of the mortal dream — animal magnetism's claim to power and reality, and the false conviction that matter and mortal mind are real. Treatment is designed to awaken you from this dream.

The greatness of Mrs. Eddy's discovery is that she has supplied us with a revelation that can replace the material viewpoint, and she has given us the form of prayer that actually brings this transformation about. As you study Christian Science, you can see that it is really most applicable to this inner level, for it supplies consciousness with a new view of God and man. As a change in this inner view flows forth and heals the upper levels, it has an awesome effect on your life.

The Healing Effect of Treatment

When working with the general treatment, even though you may not be working on some specific problem, you will find healings taking place. This daily work gently adjusts and eliminates problems without any special work being done to heal them. Such blessings come effortlessly, silently. Sometimes these healings are not immediately obvious. From time to time, you will realize that certain discordant or limiting beliefs have simply faded out. Confusion, conflicts, clashes, things going wrong, misunderstandings, accidents and other aggravations gradually cease. When you are faithful to this work, it brings more good into your life than your own human planning and effort could ever hope to achieve.

In order to realize these blessings, you must be consistent in working to discipline yourself to think in spiritual concepts until you think in them naturally. The more you practice doing this, the better your work and the better your results.

Christian Science treatment is not easy. One needs a deep desire for spiritual things in order to give a daily treatment in quiet, serious meditation. This work must be done on a consistent basis. I find when I have been away from this work for even a week or so, I have a hard time getting back to the spiritual level I had before I stopped working.

It is also important to stay with this work when there are no immediate results in the way of visible healing, or when the work is hard to do. If you are struggling with this work or realizing little healing or progress from it, you may believe that you are failing, or that you can't do it — and that you are probably the only one who is having such a struggle! Be assured that you are not alone in this. Everyone has a struggle with it!

Because we are living in a very human world and involved in a very complex society, it is not unusual, when we begin our treatment, to find we simply cannot discipline our mind to concentrate on it. At such times, it helps to read Mrs. Eddy's writings, a passage from the Bible, or an especially good article, and meditate over this in preparation for the treatment. The early Bible Lesson-Sermons are especially good as a preliminary study period before beginning your treatment. Read and ponder any of these as a free-form treatment, letting God unfold the work. It is helpful to precede treatment with a study period. Also, reading the textbook after your treatment can be very inspiring.

There are days when this work is easy; at other times, when animal magnetism is resisting it, it seems a terrible struggle. When there is such resistance to the work, you can begin with denial and handle animal magnetism vigorously before affirming the truth. While the outline of treatment is orderly, it is not rigid.

Disciplining the Mind

The time spent in treatment is not necessarily limited to an hour. I found in the beginning, as I learned to give a treatment, that it took at least an hour to go over the six footsteps.

But as I got deeper into this work, I could become so absorbed in it that I would spend many hours a day in prayer and study. I also began writing my ideas down in order to clarify them.

From this, I learned to control my mind. I developed the ability to concentrate on one thing for a long period of time. I have come to call this "thinking in a straight line." As a rule, mortal mind is undisciplined and uncontrolled. It is confused and chaotic, and lacks the ability to concentrate on one subject for any length of time. Your work in Science gives you control over your mind. You learn to concentrate and to think clearly and concisely on spiritual ideas. This alone is worth the time and effort you put into treatment, for the mental control that begins in this work is useful in all that you do.

When you practice for an hour thinking in spiritual ideas, you are training or disciplining the heart and soul and mind to live in and act out from spiritual understanding. If you persist in this, you actually come to think and live more in the spiritual view than in the material.

The Simplicity of this Work

As you progress, the treatment does not become more complex and involved. You simply understand Christian Science and pray with increasing conviction the spiritual statements you make. For example, two people, both classed as Christian Scientists, can treat a sick person in order to heal him. One can say, "God is Love and knows no sickness, and man is perfect in His likeness," and this statement can have no healing effect whatsoever because it has no meaning to the Scientist. The second Scientist may declare the very same statement and heal the patient, because he understands the statement he has made.

With increased understanding, the treatment becomes easier, clearer, more meaningful, the way one becomes more adept at mathematics or music through years of practice. Treatment is illumined and inspired by the understanding we have gained. The same simple truths are used in the same simple form of prayer, but slowly they come to have such meaning for us that we heal simply by thinking these thoughts.

Shutting out Animal Magnetism

Even under the best circumstances, the effort to treat is a challenge in the beginning. You need to approach it in a proper frame of mind. To help you do this, I am going to make a strong recommendation. Today, our lives are flooded with mortal mind beliefs, events, predictions, statistics, the latest so-called medical laws, and countless other forms of animal magnetism. This mortal mind propaganda flows out through the news media, television, movies, magazines, books. It fills people's conversations. Mortal mind talks constantly, and it talks of nothing but mortal mind.

This concentrated animal magnetism, when we take it in, leaves us distressed, worried, fearful, disturbed, agitated, and angry. It materializes the mind. Christian Scientists often absorb all of this animal magnetism because they have been told that they need to know about world conditions in order to handle them, but I do not agree that we must take it in to the most minute detail. The constant absorption of evil's mesmerism, often so graphically described and pictured, so aggressively and convincingly poured into the mind, counteracts and annuls our spirituality.

Think about this carefully. You have one mind, one focal point of thought; and you must choose where you are going to put that focal point — in the material or the spiritual viewpoint. You cannot have both in the same mind at the same time. You cannot absorb the material view through all of evil's propaganda and at the same time be convinced that it is not real. Nor can you turn spiritual thinking off and on when it suits you. After working in a treatment, you should carry these spiritual thoughts out into your daily life and live them to the highest degree possible. For this reason I urge you not to read and watch and take in the false picture that mortal mind is presenting, for it darkens your mind. If you want to spiritualize consciousness, you will protect your mind against the barrage of condensed doses of animal magnetism designed to give evil a stronger hold on you. Once aggressive suggestions have been implanted into consciousness, it is sometimes years before they fade out, and you are actually free of them.

When you fill consciousness with sensual, materialistic evil images, it prevents spiritual progress, because animal magnetism uses this mental poison to distract you and keep you from concentrating on your spiritual work each day. For the most part, you have been thinking in mortal mind for years. You have been submerged in mortal beliefs, material illusions, negative emotions, false knowledge. In a word, animal magnetism has had free reign in your consciousness. It has had its way with you unchallenged until now. When you pour the truth into consciousness, animal magnetism feels this activity. You stir it up or chemicalize it. It resists this work, and it does so in many ways. One way that it can most easily distract you, is by recalling the mesmerism that you have taken in through the media. Each time you start to pray, animal magnetism will cause you to go instead into this vast area of mortal mind impressions and think about them.

You can prevent this distraction by beginning treatment with your thought free of false images. If you have not been absorbing these aggressive suggestions, then they cannot replay themselves to you when you sit down to pray. Think about what you let into your mind, or animal magnetism will rob you of your dominion.

Remember, we think our way into the kingdom of heaven, and the greatest challenge in this mental effort is the battle with animal magnetism for control of your mind. As you discipline yourself to think in spiritual ideas, you free yourself of mortal illusions, and gain control over your own consciousness. I would not let in the animal magnetism that is flooding world consciousness today. You do not overcome animal magnetism by knowing about it, but by shutting it out, and you do this by closing off the avenues through which it tries to reach you.

How Animal Magnetism Prevents Prayer

There are many ways through which animal magnetism will try to prevent you from praying. When you begin your treatment, it will bring interruptions. It will cause your mind to wander. Instead of praying, you will spend the time rehearsing discordant events, mentally arguing with someone, regretting the past, speculating over the future, planning things to do and places to go. Animal magnetism will cause you to procrastinate. You will decide you are going to pray, but first you need to do the dishes, call some-one, pay the bills. When you try to do this work, animal magnetism will put you into a deep, very deep, sleep. When it tries to do this, walk around and wake yourself up. If the sleepiness is too much, go to sleep, then wake up and immediately take up the treatment again. Let other things go and lay aside this hour to work. As you overcome these many ways evil has of resisting its destruction, they will lessen and finally stop, and your work will be much easier.

When you make up your mind to give at least one hour a day to God, no matter what, then you learn to overcome animal magnetism and gain dominion over your consciousness. In shutting out a preoccupation with the propaganda of animal magnetism and outwitting its attempts to obstruct the treatment, you then have time and space in consciousness for cultivating the spiritual viewpoint.

The Importance of Study

The constant study of Christian Science is so necessary! You prepare for treatment through reading and study. You will need to read again and again the Bible and the writings of Mrs. Eddy. Here is the pure Word of God that shapes your work as nothing else can. To read and ponder these works is in itself a form of treatment.

In addition to the Bible and Mrs. Eddy's works, you will be greatly helped by other writings on Christian Science. There has come to light in recent years a vast treasury of books and papers on Christian Science that the Church organization in Boston withheld from Church members for decades. During the years that I was developing this work with the treatment, I did not know about these writings. I had only the 'authorized literature' approved by Boston.

I turned frequently to the pamphlets put out by the church in the 1940s and 1950s. These contained reprints of excellent articles from the periodicals. I cherished these booklets and wore them out. It was not until some years later that I discovered meta-physical writings far beyond the articles in the pamphlets. Most of this material had been written by early workers in the Cause, including Mrs. Eddy's students. I was amazed to learn that Mrs. Eddy wrote letters and articles filled with deep, pure Science. Her students also recorded her teachings. This material had never been published and made available to Christian Scientists by the Church.

I recognized these writings as the first literature of the Spiritual Age. Coupled with Mrs. Eddy's published writings, they are mankind's earliest efforts to chart the contents of the spiritual dimension and understand it. I was thrilled to find them! In 1980, as an independent Christian Scientist, I established The Bookmark in order to publish and distribute this material on Christian Science, for I felt that these writings were essential to the healing work and the prosperity of the movement.

This material is especially helpful as additional reading that helps us to understand what Mrs. Eddy has given us. Many long-time students have found these writings to be invaluable in learning how to understand and demonstrate Christian Science. They are, for the first time, able to do their own healing work.

The Serious Work of Demonstrating Christian Science

I emphasize the need to put much time and effort into the study of Christian Science because it is not a simple thing to re-form how you think. It does seem, over the years, that Christian Scientists have been led to think that spiritualizing consciousness is not really all that difficult. The healing work has been made to seem much easier than it really is. It has sometimes been said that overcoming animal magnetism can be compared to correcting a simple mistake in mathematics. But $2 + 2 = 5$ and the whole of animal magnetism are not exactly the same. It is not a quick or easy thing to disabuse the mind of mortal traits and beliefs that it has acquired over a lifetime, and discipline it to think in spiritual ideas. The spiritualization of thought comes through a total commitment to mastering the deeper teachings of Christian Science. Once you make this commitment, you should begin to realize healings. These are very encouraging signs that you are working correctly.

As you work on, however, you may also encounter unexpected trials. You may from time to time find yourself in the wilderness. Unless you understand these experiences, it would seem that Christian Science has failed you, or that you have failed Christian Science. Neither is true. The unfoldment of spiritual understanding both heals and chemicalizes your life, for this work exercises unusual influence over you and your surroundings. As you become more adept at giving a treatment, the work becomes more challenging, because it stirs your thinking and the thoughts of those closely related to you. You need to understand this in order to cope intelligently with the stirring that it produces.

Before you began working with the treatment, animal magnetism has gone unchallenged in your thinking and in the mental atmosphere around you. You might say it has been in control. It has never before been seriously threatened by the truth. When you begin to do this work, you make the truth active in consciousness and you begin to free yourself of evil's influence. You pour out the truth silently into the mental sea of minds around you. It is at this point that you learn that, in human experience, evil is not 'nothing.' As soon as animal magnetism is challenged, it begins to resist the treatment.

Evil's resistance works in many ways. It may intensify a problem so it would seem that your work is not being effective, whereas it is really being so effective that it is actually destroying evil. If you work on, facing the aggravated problem and taking your stand for truth, absolutely unintimidated by appearances, you will break the mesmerism and find healing. There are two parts to this work: one is to know the truth, and press for the demonstration; and

121

the other is to detect animal magnetism's resistance in preventing you from accomplishing this end. Evil is sly, cunning, tricky. When you begin this work, it knows that the hold it has on you is going to end, and so it fights for its life. Often this resistance is greatest at the very point where your work is about to destroy it, and you are going to realize an important healing. By pressing on and refusing to give up, you will have a victory.

There may be times when, the more you work, the more you seem to have to meet. This means, strangely enough, that the work is reaching animal magnetism and destroying it. Again, evil, so threatened, foams up and resists its own destruction. If this stirring is going on, it means that you are working correctly, and the work is being effective. If you will keep on in the face of this chemicalization and not turn back, you will overcome the error, and realize great spiritualization of thought and impressive healings.

Because the treatment is so powerful, I tell you of this, not to alarm you, but to prepare you for animal magnetism's resistance to the work. But when you are expecting healing and your challenges worsen, it is a bit disconcerting unless you know what is happening. Each day as you work with the treatment, you spiritualize your thinking and pour into the mental atmosphere around you this powerful truth. It affects you and those related to you more than you realize. It stirs up the error in this atmosphere, brings it to the surface, and causes it to pass away. This chemicalization is not easy. If it takes place, it is because this is how Truth destroys the error. These are your spiritual lessons, and you must take care not to resent them. To be sure, you probably don't deserve such struggles; but this is the way it is, and so why not accept the trial as a spiritual lesson and push on to the victory.

Each treatment you give, does something to your mind. This shifting from the material to the spiritual viewpoint brings about chemicalization both in the subjective and the objective experience. The stir can be manifested in your outer life in many ways. Stress,

conflict, discord, physical illnesses, lack — all may become intensi-
fied. Don't be put off by these challenges or this stirring. It means
you are doing very successful work. You will become experienced
in handling this stir as you continue to work. Then you will not be
intimidated by it. After awhile, you learn that the aggravation of a
problem is an excellent sign that healing of great significance is
taking place.

Rewards of Persevering

As you succeed in meeting difficult problems, wonderful
changes take place in your human experience as the result of subjective transformation. Sometimes an inner change is quite pro-
nounced. Then again, this shifting within can come about without a
strong chemicalization. Truth simply unfolds. Spiritual understanding
increases. You feel different, better, happier, freer than before. These
inner changes then move forth and change your outer life. When
dramatic external change is due to take place, it is not unusual for
one who is doing outstanding metaphysical work to fear and resist
the rearrangement of the human circumstances that he is used to.

You need to become accustomed to both inner and outer
change. In time, you realize that outer change is the fruitage of
your metaphysical work, and it always brings with it a better life.
You are pressing into a new kind of life — one lived in the spiritual
dimension. You are emerging out of mortal mind and materialism
into a more God-controlled life. Your progress brings changes
in your external life that require you to make adjustments to
new experiences. In caring for you, God does not take you beyond
what you can understand and adjust to. The outer change is the
completion of the work, and it's often quite different from what you
expected.

When inner transformation moves forth to change the outer
life, the human footsteps we are forced to take are often hard to

understand, until the demonstration is complete, and we see the results of our work. The one who does the work is the one who benefits most from it.

The Ultimate Use of Treatment

I have one more rather subtle point to share. You need to think about this idea and work with it. To me, it is the ultimate use of treatment.

Every problem, every illness, every limitation that you seem to have, is the result of a false belief in your own mind. There is no exception to this. Nothing can come into your experience unless there is something in your consciousness that lets it in. This means that the only thing in need of healing is your thinking. Over the years, I have learned to use discord, in whatever form it takes, as an indication of the need to change something within my own consciousness. I then use the problem to determine whether or not the error in my thinking has been corrected. In striving to work subjectively to detect and remove the cause of the problem, I have chosen the spiritual, rather than the human means for solving it.

When we face a challenge, the first thing we want to do is to find a human answer to it. If it is lack, we try to figure out a way to get more money. If it is a bad relationship, we have talks with the individual, or tell him off, or shut him out. If it is a painful physical problem, we treat physical pain and suffering, and we may turn to the medical profession for help, rather than searching for the mental cause.

When we use human methods, we get human results. But when we have a problem, if we gauge the outer problem to be an indication that there is something in our thinking that needs correcting, then we work from the spiritual standpoint alone. We don't try to adjust or overcome the outer problem through human methods. We pray to be shown the error in consciousness, and treat that until the error is met subjectively and a change in thought takes place. The results of this work will heal the claim permanently.

In working like this, I use the problem as a way of measuring whether or not I have really overcome the animal magnetism within. As we pray, we feel the inner change that tells us the problem is healed, even before there is any sign of it outwardly. Once this unfoldment comes, the external change will be seen as inevitable, and harmony is restored.

Accepting and Protecting your Demonstration

Your work with treatment should bring about many healings. I hope you will accept these healings with a certain casualness. Don't be surprised or impressed by them. Accept each healing with gratitude to the Father, but then go on to the next demonstration. In this way, you will always be moving from demonstration to demonstration, and this is as it should be in Christian Science. You should not be amazed by these spiritual events. They are quite natural, and you should come to expect them as the normal part of your work.

At the same time, you should protect your healings. As you come to accept them and go on, you should overcome the desire to talk much about them, or to impress others with them, or to use them to sell others on Christian Science. If you are too quick to tell about a healing, mortal mind may try to deny and reverse it. There is often the implication that it would have happened anyway.

Do be wise in talking about your demonstrations. We have very little record of Christ Jesus' personal life, and little detail by Mrs. Eddy of her own inner struggles and triumphs. I have often thought how little Mrs. Eddy wrote or talked about herself. Your own progress is between you and God. It seems best to work alone, to expect and accept your healings, and to talk very little in taking these early footsteps in the path that the Master and Mrs. Eddy pursued before us. The way for them was rugged. Because this advanced intelligence is so new, our own path will not be much easier. In time, you learn how to present Christian Science to those ready for it, and how to be still before those who will reject it.

This work is so individual that these suggestions should be adapted to your needs. You should approach treatment in a way that is best for you under your present circumstances.

Chapter XIII

HANDLING SPECIFIC PROBLEMS

When the treatment is used to meet specific problems, it is extremely effective. In this prayerful work, we look through the outer evidence and go straight to the heart of it, and handle animal magnetism with the prayer of affirmation and denial.

Many claims seem so real that they must be handled through very direct and vigorous work. There are claims that heal quickly, others must be handled over a longer period of time. Each demonstration is individual.

In handling specific claims, we cannot ignore them as though they are not there, believing that this is making nothing of error. We must recognize that there is a problem to be handled, and then take the initiative and treat it until the discord has given way and things return to normal.

Problems that need special handling take many forms. There are beliefs of flu, colds, contagious diseases; there are beliefs of accident, catastrophe, contagion, stress, things going wrong, dishonesty and crime; there are chronic false traits that produce disease and discord; there are discordant relationships, lack, age. But whatever the claim, the prayer of affirmation and denial is the basis of our prayerful work in overcoming them.

Handling Sickness and Accidents

In handling urgent claims of sickness or emergencies, the work should be taken up immediately. It should deal directly with

127

that one problem. When there is sickness, suffering, and pain, it is usually best to begin the treatment by looking through the physical picture and reducing the claim to animal magnetism. Then vehemently deny fear and the symptoms of the illness and effects of the accident. Affirm the truth about God and man. Repeat this denial and affirmation until the claim begins to improve. At this point, take up the treatment from the beginning and go through it step by step. If you are working daily for yourself, you will have spiritual strength and inspiration to draw upon. Tailor the basic steps of treatment to counteract the mesmerism producing the discord. Repeat your mental work again and again until the mesmerism is broken.

As an example of specific work, let us take a case of flu. This is a temporary belief, and would probably disappear eventually whether or not it was treated in Christian Science, but treatment can heal it quickly, even instantaneously. You can prevent a sickness or disease from developing if you are quick to deny the symptoms before they become too aggressive.

In handling such illness, this work is often most effective if you begin by denying animal magnetism with authority and aggressiveness. Insist that there is no power or reality in flu or its symptoms. There is no fear of flu or its symptoms. Declare that animal magnetism cannot make you believe in the reality of flu. It cannot make you afraid of flu. There is no cause for flu, for animal magnetism is not real. Address animal magnetism directly, and vehemently tell it, "There is no law, energy, power, or intelligence in you. There is no God in you, no mind in you. Therefore, you are to stop arguing this belief to me! You are to stop mesmerizing me! God is my life and there is no power in this suggestion or in these symptoms, and I will not fear them."

Then know that man cannot be mesmerized by this belief, for God is the only cause, and man is the perfect effect of this one divine cause. Life is health, and health is immutable, immortal. Health is a law to being. It is established by God, and is forever perfect, maintained by God, the one Mind. Man, in God's likeness, knows

128

only perfect health. He expresses freedom, vitality, and activity. God is his Life. God as cause manifests only health, and man as effect reflects only health; and you are that man!

Continue affirming the truth, and denying the symptoms until the claim is broken. Deny animal magnetism as cause and the symptoms as effect. It makes no difference that the flu seems to be manifesting itself. If you know that God is your life, then you know that your real health is intact and perfect in the one Mind. The claim is a temporal form of mesmerism and can be destroyed by your powerful statements of Truth. Truth, active in conscious-ness, will de-mesmerize thought and free you. Each statement that you make is needed to counteract the mesmerism. If you persist in arguing for Truth and against the illness, the mesmerism will give out, and you will begin to feel normal again. Your mind will be free of the mesmerism causing the illness. That is the healing, and the body will soon be free of the claim. Throughout the handling of illness, the emphasis is on denying specific aggressive mental suggestions, and affirming the truth in a very positive way.

The same type of treatment would hold true of an accident. Vehemently deny that an accident can take place in man's experience, for he is governed by the laws of God. Deny shock and all physical pain and disability. Do it quickly and with absolute con-viction that God is All. Deny that this false experience can enter thought and establish itself as a reality. Attack animal magnetism itself and deny its mental and physical cruelty. Then insist that all is well, that you are perfect right here and now. Refuse to think about the accident. Rule it out of consciousness.

Preventing Discordant Experiences

You can prevent illness, accidents, and discordant experi-ences if you refuse to entertain the belief that they are an inevitable part of man's experience. Do not accept them as happening to others. Do not rehearse such incidents or listen to anyone else do so. In your daily prayers, know that there are no accidents or discordant experiences — such as losing things, being cheated or robbed, machinery breaking down, etc. Treat your thinking daily for the aggressive suggestion that you are going to experience any kind of discord. Overcome the fear and anticipation of these things. Don't watch them on television or read about them. Don't talk about them. Actually rule out of thought the suggestion of such events coming to you. If they are not in your thinking, they cannot come into your experience. This is a spiritual law. Reduce these beliefs to aggressive mental suggestions without power or reality. Understand that in God there is only harmony, and as His reflection you think and live in harmony. Do not allow these beliefs to mesmerize you with such fear to bring them into your experience.

In your daily treatment, you can add to your denial specific claims of accident, disorder, loss, confusion, or discord. Declare that God is Life, and Life is governed by the laws of absolute intelligence and Love. This rules out discord. If you refuse to anticipate or fear accidents, theft, loss, discord, things going wrong, you will stop experiencing these things.

As you understand the mental nature of all things, you see that you cannot afford to complain, criticize, fear, discuss, or acknowledge animal magnetism, for then you are making a reality of it, and your thoughts will then move forth and cause discord in your life. You cannot pray an hour each day, and then indulge in thinking and talking mortal mind beliefs the rest of the time. You must affirm the truth throughout the day. In this way, you stop malpracticing on your own life, and that of others.

You do not have to wait until a crisis or an illness is upon you to treat specific problems. You can handle them as aggressive mental suggestions before they appear in some form of discord. Every discord begins either as your own mortal thoughts, or as the aggressive mental suggestions coming from another which you accept into consciousness. If you do not reject wrong thoughts, you will be subject to the experiences that these thoughts produce. As you succeed in shutting out the thoughts that produce sickness and discord, the manifestation of these beliefs will lessen until they disappear from your experience.

Chronic Claims

Christian Science can heal chronic or incurable physical problems, because all disease has a mental cause. There is no exception to this fact. Disease begins with ignorant or intentional disobedience to God's laws.

If you examine your thinking and emotions, you will detect mental disobedience in yourself. When I was in the practice, I had cases — some of them very serious cases — where the patient refused to believe that there was any mental disobedience to God in his consciousness. This was mental blindness. If he were that perfect, he wouldn't have the problem. We all have mortal traits and beliefs to overcome. Instead of resisting the need to transform consciousness, we should humbly accept the work of recognizing and casting out wrong or sinful thought-habits.

In handling false traits, you are working on specific mental causes that produce disease. As you define man in spiritual terms, a new image of man unfolds. Then daily deny ungodlike traits in yourself, and work to conform to this image. Through this inner transformation, you identify with the real image of man and individualize it. It becomes you. You think in it. You live it. You come to know yourself in God's likeness.

Handling false traits heals physical problems that cannot be healed in any other way. Remember that animal magnetism uses matter as a subterfuge. It causes us to blame heart problems and skin problems and migraine headaches and cancer on matter and its laws. But all sickness and disease are the end result of chronic wrong thinking. Often the sin or wrong thinking has been going on

131

for weeks, months, even a lifetime before the physical claim appeared, and so we do not necessarily relate the mental cause to the physical claim. In your daily work, identify with your declarations of the truth about man and cast out mortal traits. Then you have overcome the cause of the problem, and it is healed permanently.

The synonym Love is especially helpful in analyzing and changing the innermost thoughts and feelings. False traits are emotions — fear, self-will, hatred, personal sense, anger, self-justification, self-love, etc. These negative emotions are the opposite of Love, and so we have a way to gauge how well our inner self relates to God. We can compare it to Love and its attributes. In all that we think and say and do, we should ask ourselves, Is it loving?

The synonym Love includes patience, forgiveness, humility, gentleness, kindness, compassion, understanding, tenderness, temperance, loveliness, graciousness, generosity, purity, thoughtfulness, unselfishness, spiritual affection. It takes great mental discipline to express these qualities to everyone all the time.

In your treatment, work with Love. Deny the traits that are not loving, and make the supreme effort to be loving in daily relationships. The real test is living love moment by moment. When you are alone, you must think loving thoughts. Then when you are faced with unkind, difficult, aggravating situations, you must prove this love by being loving, kind, forgiving, patient, understanding.

It takes tremendous strength to be patient and forgiving to everyone all the time, but when you do, you are refusing to be a channel for animal magnetism's harmful, hateful emotions. Animal magnetism controls us more through these negative emotions than in any other way. How quick we are to react when we feel abused or misunderstood! How often we secretly harbor antagonism, resentment, disapproval, hurt feelings! In our treatment each day, we should handle these false emotions. We can forgive. We can refuse to think or say unkind, critical things. We can be patient and understanding. In demonstrating these spiritual qualities, we overcome negative emotions that sooner or later are the cause of stubborn, seemingly incurable claims.

As you cultivate spiritual love, you leave behind discordant, sickness-producing traits, for you can not have both in the same mind at the same time. You must choose. Actually — you must choose to be loving! This greatly simplifies the work of overcoming mortal traits. Your intuitions tell you when you are being loving and when you are not.

Study the synonym, Love, relate to it, live it, for spiritual love lived is the scientific method of healing incurable claims.

Demonstrating Harmonious Relationships

Human relationships are too often an endless source of conflict, anger, hatred, disappointment, hurt, resentment, and frustration. We are sometimes told in Christian Science that if we are loving to everyone, they will be loving to us; and that if we have a relationship problem, all we have to do is straighten out *our* thinking and harmony will prevail. I have not found this to be entirely true. If we are unwise in how we love, we simply become a doormat for those who are dominating, selfish, and difficult. In order to have harmonious relationships, we should demonstrate them, and we do this as we spiritualize consciousness.

Recall that your thinking moves forth to shape your life. This is as true of your relationships as it is of your health or success. We usually believe that certain people are the cause of our difficulties. If they would just straighten out or leave us alone, our lives would be happier. But difficult relationships are due to mortal elements in our own mental makeup that draw them into our experience.

If you seem to have inharmonious relationships, and all of these 'difficult people' were removed from your experience, they would soon be replaced by others who were just as difficult, because your inner self has not changed. These people are part of your experience because your mental state attracts them to you.

You will have better relationships, as you uncover the negative traits within and replace them with the qualities of Love. As with other challenges, you are concerned only with your own inner self. As your own thinking is spiritualized, either your relationships improve or they fall away.

We all long to have a gentle, kind, gracious, warm, honest, intelligent circle of family and friends. But unless we embody these qualities ourselves, we will not attract such people to us. In fact, such a person may come our way, and we will not know it because our mortal selfhood prevents us from recognizing and appreciating the spiritual nature of this individual.

As you reflect more and more of your true selfhood in God's likeness, this will bring about harmonious relationships with those that respond to this work, and it will gently remove those that do not — if you let this adjustment take place.

Sometimes we hear it said that we must remain in a discordant situation until we have healed it, that to leave, rather than stay and 'work it out,' is considered failure in resolving the problem in Science. But this is not a scientific solution for some relationships. Such human outlining can prevent us from making the demonstration of better relationships. At times, we may associate with those who have very difficult, disagreeable dispositions, and they may have no intention of changing. We can become very discouraged in attempting to have a kind relationship with them. Furthermore, if we remain in contact with them for any length of time, the animal magnetism handling them could seem to handle us.

You do not have to let animal magnetism come in the form of aggressive, demanding acquaintances who intrude on your life and demand that you endure mortal mind talk, mortal mind abuse. This can paralyze your unfoldment and growth. Take your stand with this belief, just as you would with any other form of animal magnetism. Specifically handle it in your own consciousness.

We should reach the place in our prayerful work when we no longer react to mortal mind, when we can stand absolutely unintimidated by the animal magnetism handling others, and we can do this as we learn that such animal magnetism is not of God. When we can do this, either the relationship will improve or we will be lifted out of it. The demonstration may lead to a dissolving of the relationship. Mrs. Eddy writes, "Wisdom will ultimately put asunder what she hath not joined together." If we are progressing spiritually and the other individual is not, the relationship could more or less end. Often this comes about harmoniously.

We learn in Christian Science that we do not have to endure hateful relationships. There has been a theory among Christian Scientists that we must persist with people who are hateful, dominating, argumentative, willful, manipulative, materialistic, in order to heal them. While we should offer a cup of cold water to those who might be receptive to Christian Science, we do not have to sacrifice our own spiritual growth by holding on to those who vehemently oppose Science. There are many people today who are not ready for Christian Science, and we do not have to subject ourselves to the mental abuse of those who are antagonistic towards it in hopes of reaching and reforming them. This can retard our own demonstration without helping them in any way. If we are progressing spiritually, God removes such people from our experience, and He teaches us how to work wisely in presenting Christian Science to those ready for it.

Do work metaphysically to demonstrate happy relationships. This is part of your spiritual development. In Christian Science, we do not eliminate relationships; we spiritualize them.

Overcoming Limited Supply

Often Christian Scientists will handle sickness, accidents, discordant relationships, but seldom do they try to overcome limited supply by understanding the infinite spiritual resources at hand. They continually struggle with financial needs because they believe conditions external to consciousness control their supply. Actually, all lack and limitation are as much a form of mesmerism as are sickness and discord, and they can be handled subjectively by breaking down the fear of lack.

If you are having financial difficulties, challenge this belief and overcome it. Limited income is a universal belief that will limit the good you have for a lifetime, unless you take the initiative and handle it as a specific claim.

Handling Age and the Past

We cannot begin too soon handling the belief of age. The belief in a mortal past, a beginning and an end to life, has many causes: the universal belief in mental and physical aging; heredity; the accumulation of unsolved problems; the belief in passing time; malpractice. Our work in Science helps us to counteract all of these causes.

But specific work on the belief of age can go on constantly. Resist the suggestion of growing old. Don't anticipate it as inevitable. Don't talk age, or accept it for yourself or others. Do not wait until the symptoms of age begin to manifest themselves. Handle it now, and handle it often. Do much preventive work on it through the study of the synonym Life, with its many attributes.

It is also good to handle the past. Animal magnetism uses the past to fasten the belief of age on us. See that life is indestructible, always unfolding, always progressing. The experiences of the past can teach us many spiritual lessons; but once we have learned them, we should forget the unfortunate part of the past, and not keep rehearsing wrongs and misfortunes. Mortal events of the past accumulate to produce age.

Regard a mortal past as animal magnetism, and know that animal magnetism alone experienced it, suffered from it, and remembers it. Then refuse to be drawn into the habit of ruminating over the past. This is mesmerism. Refuse to think about it. Turn away from the past and live in the eternal now. Reject the belief that man has a mortal past. If you will do this, disturbing memories will stop coming to you. This will help you to overcome the belief of birth, age and death.

Demonstrating Intelligence

Christ Jesus used advanced intelligence which he made practical in the human realm. His demonstrations were not guesswork or faith healings. They were the result of his understanding of God made evident in human experience. Through the study of Christian Science, we begin to reflect this same intelligence.

Animal magnetism claims we have a limited intelligence. In Christian Science, we learn that everyone has unlimited intelligence. The mesmeric belief of limited intelligence needs to be broken. Affirm that your ability to understand Christian Science is from God, and therefore you do not have a limited intelligence. Your mind reflects infinite Mind, and so you can know all things. Declare daily that you can understand Christian Science. Then expect to!

As you treat your intelligence, you feel it expanding. The spiritual ideas which unfold give you wisdom and understanding concerning spiritual things. In your daily treatment, you are developing an advanced intelligence. As you press deeper and deeper into Christian Science, you understand the method of prayer that enables you to heal. You know how to affirm spiritual facts, attack animal magnetism and heal yourself. This alone is a powerful form of intelligence. Your understanding of Christian Science will continue to grow as you pray daily for yourself. Each unfoldment, each healing experience, is a learning time. You do not keep repeating the same work, any more than a mathematician keeps reviewing addition. Your intelligence expands as you spiritualize consciousness.

This expansion of intelligence is not confined to spiritual unfoldment. It is manifested in all avenues of your life: your business, home, relationships, activities, talents, skills. If you work to develop spiritual intelligence first, other learning will be much easier. I make a point of the need to demonstrate intelligence, because this is not stressed enough in Christian Science. Great emphasis is placed on learning to love, and rightly so. But intelligence is equally important.

Through prayer, we reflect divine intelligence, creative intelligence, and practical intelligence. We also demonstrate the opportunity to express it freely. There are times when thwarted or suppressed intelligence is more painful than unrequited love. This work not only develops your intellectual capacity, but it opens the avenues for greater opportunity and fulfillment.

Humility Essential

Spiritual understanding comes from the unfoldment of spiritual ideas as we listen within for them. We cannot contrive or devise these ideas out of human consciousness. They come from God. They illumine consciousness and bring healing. It takes humility to discern these ideas and retain them. However much you learn and demonstrate Christian Science, do remain humble! Mrs. Eddy tells us that humility is the genius of Christian Science. So often, I have sadly watched very capable, healing Christian Scientists being led astray through egotism — a puffed-up self-importance that eventually clouds over their ability to heal.

Remember always, that these spiritual talents, these divine ideas, are gifts from God. Egotism, pride, self-love, judging others self-righteously — all of this paralyzes spiritual growth. If animal magnetism can possibly handle you through pride and egotism, it will. Watch for this. Christ Jesus said, "I can of mine own self do nothing." Try to demonstrate and live humility.

Obeying the Ethics of Christian Science

I want to add another word of warning. You should do this mental work for *yourself alone*. Stay out of other people's minds. Do not treat another without his consent. There are exceptions to this rule, but very few. This work is so powerful that you do not always understand the effect you have on others if you decide to quietly do a little prayerful work for them. This is a violation of the ethics of Christian Science. It will so darken your mind that you will lose your ability to heal.

Many times I have seen an abuse of mental power when someone does silent mental work for another without his permission, or attempts to mentally manipulate him without his knowing it. Those who do this become malpractitioners, and they believe that no one knows of their disobedience to the ethics of Science. But they forget that God knows, and He forbids this, even when it is done from the highest sense of human goodness and the most unselfish motives.

The development of this advanced intelligence does not give anyone the license to abuse or misuse it. I tell you this to protect you from the terrible mental darkness that comes to those who ignorantly or maliciously use this power to pray for or influence another secretly.

CONCLUSION

The spiritual dimension is different from the mortal realm. It is a holy realm. Christian Science does not make you a better human being more involved in a better material world. It makes you different. You eventually think in a different dimension as you discern the spiritual nature of man and the universe. You know to some extent that the spiritual dimension is right here, right now. You begin to live in it as this dimension becomes as real and tangible to you as the material one is to others. You begin to emerge out of the world of materialism and sensualism into divine reality. You have control over your life, because you can control your thinking.

In this demonstration of spiritual understanding, the treatment is everything. It is the most powerful form of intelligence on earth. I have seen it move mental mountains, control the weather, prevent death, overcome entrenched mortal beliefs and insurmountable problems, heal incurable disease, bring supply where no avenue for it was visible, protect from terrible catastrophe, and renovate the entire structure of the inner and outer world. In time, those who learn to demonstrate Christian Science know that truly, "all things are possible to God."

In this discussion, I have shared with you the prayer that will enable you to begin this wonderful adventure into the spiritual dimension — the treatment. And now, the rest is up to you!

APPENDIX

The following citations, from the writings of Mary Baker Eddy, are for use in the study of each chapter.

Abbreviations for Mrs. Eddy's books:

S&H	Science and Health with Key to the Scriptures
Mis	Miscellaneous Writings
Ret	Retrospection and Introspection
Pul	Pulpit and Press
Un	Unity of Good
Rud	Rudimental Divine Science
No	No and Yes
Pan	Christian Science versus Pantheism
'00	Message to The Mother Church for 1900
'01	Message to The Mother Church for 1901
'02	Message to The Mother Church for 1902
Hea	Christian Healing
Peo	The People's Idea of God
My	The First Church of Christ, Scientist, and Miscellany

Chapter II : The Spiritual Age

S&H
124: 3-13
134: 14-15
268: 1-13
380: 22-28
546: 23-26
573: 3-28

'00
4: 11-15

Peo
1: 2-2

My
158: 9-10

Chapter IV: The Material and Spiritual Viewpoint

S&H

123: 11-15	337: 20-28
167: 20-26	355: 32-8
209: 16-30	481: 7-12
269: 29-10	
288: 3-14	Ret
300: 13-22	59: 18-10
306: 21-25	

Chapter V: The Prayer of Affirmation and Denial

S&H

1: 1-14	Mis
4: 3-5	127: 7-19
11: 27-32	
14: 31-24	No
418: 22-25	38:25 to 40:13
	Peo
	9:22-26

Chapter VI: Footsteps One and Two of a General Treatment

God

S&H

116: 20-23	228: 25-27
140: 4-12	267: 5-6
205: 12-13	275: 12-14
213: 9-10	287: 13-16 (continued)

S&H	Rud
331:1 1-8	1:5-9
465: 8-6	
472: 24-26 (All)	My
473: 7-10	149: 5-13
492: 25-28	
517: 22-24	
519: 25-28	
587: 5-8	

Chapter VII: The Synonyms

Principle

S&H
112: 32-3
284: 11-12
318: 28-30
588: 9-21

Mind

S&H
  2: 23-25
 70: 12-13
114: 10-11
151: 26-28
187: 22-24
191: 32-1
206: 28-31209: 5-8
209: 5-8
239: 29-30
259: 26-31

280: 1-8
283: 4-7
284: 8-10
291: 13-18
379: 6-8
468: 10-11
469: 12-17
505: 9-12
510: 27-6
591: 16-20

Soul

S&H
 60: 29-3
 71: 7-9
247: 10-2
306: 7-8
310: 11-2
467: 17-23
481: 28-29

Spirit

S&H
 70: 5-8
 71: 1-2; 5-9
 89: 20-21
109: 32-7
170: 22-27
250: 7-11
278: 1-11
300: 23-31
468: 11-24
480: 1-5
507: 3-7

Life

S&H
 76: 22-29
289: 32-2
331: 1-10
347: 6-7
487: 3-6, 27-29

Truth

S&H
 67: 23-24
123: 30-2
183: 23-29
282: 26-27

S&H
287: 32-2
293: 28-31
299: 24-30
367: 30-9
474: 31-2

Love

S&H
 6: 17-18
 19: 6-11
113: 5-8
201: 17-19
224: 31
225: 21-22
340: 12-14
494: 10-14

Mis
 8: 8 to 13:12
249: 27 to 250:29
312: 2-9

'02
 4: 18 to 9:17
 11: 6-9

Chapter VIII: Man and the Universe

Man	*The Universe*
S&H	S&H
42: 19-20	83: 13-20
63: 5-11	118: 26-32
90: 30-32	124: 14-31
94: 1-6	191: 21-23
200: 16-19	209: 10-11
209: 1-2	240: 1-17
250: 7-13	256: 5-8
258: 25-21	264: 20-21
265: 1-5	272: 28-30
273: 18-20	295: 5-8
280: 25-30	427: 23-25
288: 31-1	503: 10-17
290: 25-27	513: 6-13
294: 25-27	520: 16-3
302: 14-24	536: 1-9
305: 5-11	550: 5-7
317: 16-20	555: 22-23
336: 9-18	585: 5-8
372: 14-17	
427: 1-7	Mis
428: 22-29	21: 1 to 30:32
475: 5-31	190: 1-10
476: 28-8	331: 22-5
591: 5-7	364: 10-21

Rud
4:6-18 (continued)

Universe (continued)
My
106: 15-16
129: 10-14

149:5-13
226:6-20

Chapter IX: Fourth Footstep: Handling Animal Magnetism

Matter

S&H
 97: 11-20, 26-28
118: 26-16
171: 25-30
173: 6-16
182: 32-7
264: 21 (only)
273: 1-9, 21-28
276: 31-2
277: 24-32
281: 4-6
282: 23-25
287: 24-27
293: 3-12
294: 9-24
310: 1-6
369: 5-13
372: 3-13, 22-24
477: 9-18
478: 20-27
479: 8-17
504: 27-3
543: 28-30
591:8 -15 (continued)

Rud
 4: 19 to 6:2

Mortal Mind

S&H
 70: 1-5
 86: 29-31
 91: 9-21
114: 1-9, 12-17
144: 8-26
171: 17-22
178: 18-27
186: 28-12
188: 4-10
206: 4-13
212: 17-18
242: 15-20
260: 22-30
262: 27-32
270: 24-30
289: 2-11
295: 19-3 (continued)

Mortal Mind	*Animal Magnetism*
S&H	S&H
299: 31-8	71: 2-4
310: 29-6	93: 13-20
318: 9-15	101: 21-8
328: 4-13	102: 30-31
337: 5-7	103: 17-2
339: 7-19	104: 13-18
359: 29-21	186: 11-27
385: 31-4	192: 24-26
391: 24-28	207: 8-13
396: 26-7	252: 7-14
398: 23-24	287: 22-23
399: 16 to 400:29	311: 8-13
402: 8-15	330: 25-32
403: 16-20	448: 5-11
404: 9-12, 29-17	469: 25-28
418: 13-16	474: 26-29
425: 14-17	537: 14-18
430: 3-5	539: 3-7
462: 20-27	564: 24-5
476: 9-22	584: 17-25
478: 23-26	
505: 28-2	Mis
536: 24-29	123: 3-7
544: 14-15	284: 24-28
545: 7-10, 32-3	346: 6-21
554: 4-7	
556: 10-13	Pan
569: 3-5	11: 20-27 (continued)

APPENDIX

Animal Magnetism

No
Ret
23: 18-2
 67: 1-5

Unity of Good: entire book

My
210: 18 to 213: 26

Chapter X: Affirm the Oneness of God and Man

S&H
284: 28-32

476: 4-5
477: 29-2
502: 24-27

303: 25-2
306: 8-10
361: 16-20
470: 21-5

Chapter XII: The Purpose and Power of a General Treatment

S&H
 10: 1-4, 6-8
 16: 1-2
 19: 24-28
 22: 20-22
 40: 31-7
 66: 1-16, 31-3
 90: 27-30
130: 15-20
162: 9-11
168: 30-9
174: 9-16
181: 12-13

208: 20-24
209: 31-32
232: 26-7
234: 26-3
238: 19-21
240: 18-4
264: 24-31
296: 4-21
322: 26-18
390: 32-16
410: 14-21
425: 21-28
426: 9-11

428: 8-12, 15-21
462: 13-19
485: 14-19
496: 15-19
519: 28-2
536: 26-29
540: 5-16
548: 12-17
552: 16-19
571: 15-19
586: 23-25
597: 16-19

Mis
15: 4 to 20: 5
118: 16-28
154: 23-2
203: 1 to 207: 6
267: 22-2
306: 22-9
323: 1 to 328: 32

'00
2: 7-8
'02
19: 15-9

Peo
7: 30-3

My
126: 28-3
149: 31-4
159: 12-24
202: 27-28
210: 1-17
244: 15-19

Ann Beals is a life-long Christian Scientist. Her family came into Christian Science through a healing she had before she was a year old. Doctors could not diagnose the illness or cure it. She seemed about to pass on when her mother called in a Christian Science practitioner who prayed for her until she regained consciousness. Within a short time she was completely healed. Her parents then took up the study of Christian Science and the family attended First Church of Christ, Scientist in Louisville, Kentucky. During her early years she had several healings of extremely serious illnesses through reliance on Christian Science. In time her father, Harry Smith, became a Christian Science teacher and lecturer.

While attending Washington University in St. Louis, Missouri, Ms. Beals met and married Robert Beals. They had two sons, Charles and John. After serving the branch church in Decatur, Georgia, in many ways, she became a Christian Science practitioner, listed in *The Christian Science Journal*. She also contributed a number of articles to the Christian Science periodicals.

Early in her practice work, she realized the need for writings that explained more fully how to demonstrate Christian Science. But when she submitted deeper articles to the editors of the periodicals, they were unwilling to publish them.

As she watched the steady decline of the Christian Science Church, her concern for the future of the movement led her, in 1974, to publish independently of the Church organization her booklet *Animal Magnetism*. Because of Church policy, members of the Church, and especially *Journal* listed practitioners, were forbidden to publish writings without the permission of the Christian Science Board of Directors. After publishing her booklet, she was forced to resign her *Journal* listing as a practitioner.

In 1975, she met Reginald G. Kerry. He shared her deep concern about the decline in the Church. His work at Church headquarters in Boston had led him to see that the decline in the Church was largely due to the immorality and corruption at Church headquarters. He delivered an ultimatum to the Board of Directors that they either "clean up things at headquarters" or he would write Church members exposing the corruption and immorality there. When the Board refused to take his threat seriously, he carried out his promise to "write the field." Ms. Beals assisted him in sending the Kerry Letters. For two years, while living in Boston, she worked with him in getting out the first four Kerry Letters. Her book, *Crisis In the Christian Science Church*, tells of these events.

After mailing the fourth Kerry Letter, she moved to California. She resigned from the Church in 1977. She continued assisting the Kerrys in sending out the Letters. In 1980, she started The Bookmark with the conviction that the time had come when deeper writings on Christian Science had to be published and made available to everyone. As this work has progressed, she has been able to publish and promote many profound works on Christian Science that have been suppressed by the Board of Directors over the years.

She presently lives in Santa Clarita, California, where she continues to write papers on Christian Science, and serve as publisher and editor of The Bookmark.

For further information regarding Christian Science:
Write: The Bookmark
        Post Office Box 801143
        Santa Clarita, CA 91380
Call: 1-800-220-7767
Visit our website: www. thebookmark.com